More Praise for *Beyond th*

MW00779702

"James Harris's latest work on preaching is a gift to all preachers who take the biblical text seriously in the preparation of their sermons. While there are many how-to books on preaching, few can match the wisdom, insight, and skill that Harris brings to the interpretive task. Harris argues that 'getting in front of the text' will create a new paradigm for preaching—one that opens the way to new understandings of scripture. This book is a wonderful addition to the great craft of African American preaching. It will rightly join the ranks of excellent works on this much beloved preaching tradition."

—Cleophus J. LaRue, Francis Landey Patton Professor of Homiletics, Princeton Theological Seminary, Princeton, NJ

"James Harris has done it again. *Beyond the Tyranny of the Text* offers a profoundly liberative reading of Ricoeur's work while being deeply grounded in historic practices of Black biblical interpretation. Given Harris's rich insight, preaching will be the better for it!"

—David Schnasa Jacobsen, professor of the practice of homiletics; director, Homiletical Theology Project; Boston University School of Theology, Boston, MA

"Dr. Harris treats preaching as a creative art and process that entails both the cognitive and the emotive, and he offers a new and more effective hermeneutical tool he calls 'proclaiming in front of the text.' His emphasis on the type of proclamation that takes seriously the reading, re-reading, and un-reading of the biblical text are helpful not only in conceiving but also in constructing and delivering sermons. This book is a *vade mecum* for those who are interested in finding their way through both the fundamentals and the complexities of preaching."

—Lewis Baldwin, professor emeritus of religious studies, Vanderbilt University, Nashville, TN

James Henry Harris

BEYOND
the
TYRANNY
of
the
TEXT

Preaching in Front of the Bible to Create a New World

Abingdon Press
Nashville

BEYOND THE TYRANNY OF THE TEXT:
PREACHING IN FRONT OF THE BIBLE TO CREATE A NEW WORLD

Copyright © 2019 by James Henry Harris

All rights reserved.

No part of this work may be reproduced or transmitted in any form or by any means, electronic or me-chanical, including photocopying and recording, or by any information storage or retrieval system, except as may be expressly permitted by the 1976 Copyright Act or in writing from the publisher. Requests for permission should be addressed to Permissions, Abingdon Press, 2222 Rosa L. Parks Boulevard, Nashville, TN 37228-1306, or permissions@abingdonpress.com.

LCCN: 2019948357

ISBN 978-1-5018-8906-6

Scripture unless otherwise noted is from the Common English Bible. Copyright © 2011 by the Common English Bible. All rights reserved. Used by permission. www.CommonEnglishBible.com.

Scripture marked (KJV) is from The Authorized (King James) Version. Rights in the Authorized Version in the United Kingdom are vested in the Crown. Reproduced by permission of the Crown's patentee, Cambridge University Press.

Scripture marked (NIV) is taken from the Holy Bible, New International Version®, NIV®. Copyright © 1973, 1978, 1984, 2011 by Biblica, Inc.™ Used by permission of Zondervan. All rights reserved world-wide. www.zondervan.com The "NIV" and "New International Version" are trademarks registered in the United States Patent and Trademark Office by Biblica, Inc.™

Scripture marked (NKJV) is taken from the New King James Version®. Copyright © 1982 by Thomas Nelson. Used by permission. All rights reserved.

Scriptures marked (NRSV) is taken from the New Revised Standard Version Bible, copyright © 1989 Na-tional Council of the Churches of Christ in the United States of America. Used by permission. All rights reserved worldwide. http://nrsvbibles.org/.

19 20 21 22 23 24 25 26 27 28—10 9 8 7 6 5 4 3 2 1
MANUFACTURED IN THE UNITED STATES OF AMERICA

Dedicated to my wife, Demetrius,
sons, James Corey Alexander and Cameron Christopher David Harris,
and to my brothers, John (deceased), Douglas, Horace, Emerson (deceased), and Glenn,
and my sisters, Gloria (deceased), Jackie, Marianna (deceased), and Venessa,
whose love for preaching has blessed me beyond measure.

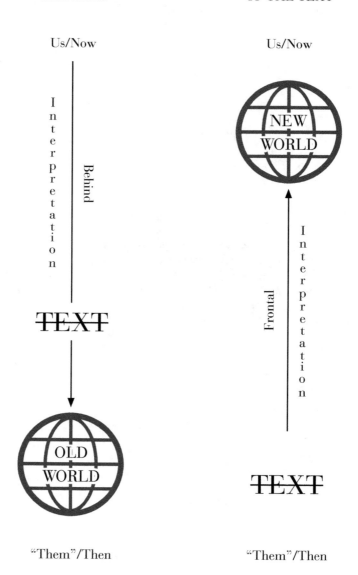

CONTENTS

Contents

CHAPTER FIVE: RE-WRITING/PREACHING—
A New Method of Interpretation

FOREWORD

The book you are now reading moves between Jonah and Jesus, practice and theory, dangerous meditations on the art of preaching and urgent meditations on contemporary life. Its title led me to imagine two photographs. Both suggest the theme James Henry Harris pursues: we discover the meanings we preach not *behind the text* but *in front of it*. What can that mean?

First image: a cassocked minister stands in her pulpit or behind a lectern. The wide-angle lens capturing the scene is just above and behind her shoulder. We see the text—an open Bible, sermon notes, or both—and we see people in the pews, listening, responding. Where, literally, in this picture, is the meaning?

Second image: now the preacher is in shirt-sleeves, in her study, gazing on a street outside the window. Just behind her is the desk from which she has just turned. It is buried deep under stacks of reference books, lexicons, newspapers, and a laptop. In the middle are Bibles of various translations laying open, all to the same passage, which appears on the computer screen as well, perhaps in Greek. Where, in this photograph, is the meaning of the text?

Several answers occurred to me, but, as I read, I saw how Harris suggests that none of my answers would be satisfactory by itself. In the first picture, one might focus on either the text or the people, and answer that the meaning must be "in" one or the other. The meaning might be "inside" the text itself, the biblical text or the sermon text. Text and meaning would be identical. No "in front." No "behind." The text simply means what it says: "The Spirit of the Lord is upon me, because he has anointed me to bring good news to the poor" (Luke 4:18a NRSV).

On the other hand, one might say that there is no meaning anywhere apart from actual human minds that make or receive meaning. In the first photograph, we see the people hearing the sermon. The sermon is for them, and the meaning must be "in" their minds as they hear and respond. "Today this scripture has been fulfilled *in your hearing*" (4:21, emphasis added).

The second picture offers another possibility for "where" meaning is. For centuries, historians and theologians have worried about both the opaqueness of the biblical text and the obtuseness of hearers and readers of the word. In Luke 4, scripture is quoting scripture, so which scripture is being fulfilled: Isaiah's or Luke's? And in whose hearing: the people in the ancient synagogue or the people in the preacher's church? What is more, before Jesus tried to explain himself by citing even more scripture, the people were at first "amazed" (v. 22). But later "all in the synagogue were filled with rage" (v. 28) and tried to toss him off a cliff! Why?

To these sorts of issues, we are told we need to get "behind" the text— to its context, history, language, geography, society, and culture, as well as to traditions of Jewish, Christian, and Muslim interpretation. Hence, behind the open Bibles in my imagined photograph are reference books, translation aids, and guides for studying the times of the text and the signs of the times—signs the pastor watches for out the window. However, where is the meaning really: behind the text or out the window?

To this question, Harris takes a clue from the French hermeneutical philosopher and frequent biblical interpreter Paul Ricoeur (1913–2005). The meaning is not the same as the text's linguistic structure. Nor is it hiding in the minds of the original author or audience, which can never be completely known. Ricoeur writes, "The sense of a text is not behind the text, but in front of it. It is not something hidden, but something disclosed."[1] As we hear the text's sentences, they project before us a new relationship of meaning, pointing toward the world and inviting us to think in new directions.

---

1. Paul Ricoeur, *Interpretation Theory: Discourse and the Surplus of Meaning* (Fort Worth: Texas Christian University Press, 1973), 87.

In the first photo, this new relationship of meaning surrounds both the preacher in the pulpit and the congregation in the pews. In the second, the biblical text is directing the pastor's gaze from the page to the world—as if the pages of the Bible and the commentaries were turning her head and bending her heart toward homes and streets outside her window. Is it too much to suggest that meaning from the text is *liberating* her from her study, even from her pulpit, and the congregants from their pews? Harris is saying that before a text can liberate us, we must place our minds and bodies in front of it. We must get to where it—the text—can affect and move us, disclosing new and liberating directions for living and valuing.

My imagination is still stuck on the second photo. Those commentaries, dictionaries, and annotated translations give me pause. We all study them, if we ever preach sermons—at least we all should. I have contributed to some myself, and I know that, at least twice, ministers have read what I wrote! (Okay, one of the ministers was my sister.) My hope here is that James Harris will not be misconstrued. He is not marginalizing biblical scholarship, and he is not making sermon preparation any easier. Rather, he is trying to liberate preaching from two kinds of reduction.

One kind is associated with Biblicism or even fundamentalism, which treats biblical passages like data points with single meanings. True, the likely readers of this book or *The Interpreter's Bible* may not be susceptible to this sort of reductionism, but even the most broad-minded of us can be blinded by narrow views of a text. Imagine you have been brooding over Luke's account of Jesus in the synagogue. "The Spirit of the Lord...has sent me to proclaim release to the captives and recovery of sight to the blind, to let the oppressed go free, to proclaim the year of the Lord's favor" (4:18b). And you are strangely moved to compose a fascinating sermon on whether "the Spirit" refers to the Holy Spirit, to be sent at Pentecost (Acts 2:1-4), or the spirit of God hovering over the waters (Gen 1:2). Meanwhile, outside, the oppressed are still listening for word of the liberating favor of the Lord.

There is another kind of reductionism that worries Harris more, namely, reducing the biblical text to explanations of the text, that is to say, reducing the living word to commentary. Again, he finds Ricoeur helpful.

For Ricoeur, written discourse is lively—indeed, it seems almost alive. To read a text attentively is to hear it speaking, even upon first reading. When I open to Luke 4—"He stood up to read, and the scroll of the prophet Isaiah was given to him. He unrolled the scroll and found the place where it was written: 'The Spirit of the Lord is upon me...'"—and immediately I *understand something*, or not. Maybe not, but I probably will *sense* that, to some extent, the text is addressing me. For Ricoeur, a philosopher of language, this much is minimally true of *any text*. Anything we can read has the potential to address us, for better or worse. Luke 4 is especially pertinent, for it depicts a scene of reading, interpreting, and responding.

For Ricoeur to say more, of how this text engages us as *scripture* or revelation, will involve other considerations—of symbol, metaphor, narrative, and especially the relation between manifestation and proclamation.[2] But for now, Harris wants us to pay attention to how even on first reading, the "sense" is actually "in front" of the text, moving toward us. The sense projected by the text is already engaging our feelings and understanding, even if only minimally.

At this early point in our reading or hearing, our understanding may be relatively accurate, or else quite puzzling, or misleading. Even so, those are all ways of being engaged. To say "I don't understand!" is to ask a question and to be questioned, and so is already to be in a process of understanding. Our confusing questions can be good; they signal we are caught up in the text. Now is time to consult those dictionaries and commentaries.

However, now is also a time, Harris thinks, when things can go wrong—and sometimes go wrong by going right. For in a very important way, it *is* the job of scholarship to "get behind the text." Ricoeur calls getting behind the text "explanation," which is the counterpart to "understanding." Interpretation, for Ricoeur, is a dialectical motion, a back and forth interplay between felt understanding and informed explanation.

---

2. See the essay "Manifestation and Proclamation" in Paul Ricoeur, *Figuring the Sacred: Religion, Narrative, and Imagination* (Minneapolis: Fortress, 1995).

For instance, the notes in any good annotated Bible will direct you to the Isaiah passages Jesus is quoting (61:1-2, 58:6), and the notes may also comment on how Luke reflects Jewish practices of reading and teaching scripture in first-century synagogues. Only Luke records Jesus quoting Isaiah here, although Matthew and Mark also mention his visit to Nazareth and the controversy that followed. So Luke—and possibly his audience—most likely had a special interest in the Isaiah passage. Historical commentaries may also discuss the growing, perhaps subversive importance of synagogue worship in Roman-occupied Palestine about the time the Roman destroyed the temple in 70 CE, not long before Luke came to be written. One could go on and on, for ink in countless libraries and clouds of websites continues to rain insight upon the Bible.

Typically, two good things happen to the interpreter who consults such reference works: uncertainties are explained, and new understandings are suggested. At best, explanation becomes an *occasion* for richer understanding, but—for Ricoeur and Harris—explanation is not the same as understanding, which is always more mysterious. At best, understanding gets us started; explanation clarifies, corrects, and redirects; and the text points us toward a new, richer understanding of the world. At worst, we become too interested in the commentaries or get sidelined by their academic authority, even to the point of missing the text altogether or limiting its range of meaning. That is what worries Harris.

The best analogy I can think of for the mysterious, dialectical motion of understanding and explanation in preaching is from music. Now, understand, I do not read music. When, rarely, I can decipher the notes, they do not sound in my head as written words do. Yet, for as long I can remember, passages from Bach and Beethoven have thrilled me, bodily and intellectually, and I have been learning to love moments from Gustav Mahler and John Coltrane. In a sense, I "understand" their music, but I do not know "why." So I keep pestering my musical friends with why questions, like, "Why do I enjoy minor keys?" and "What does a minor key 'do'?" Often, their answers really help.

To extend this analogy, imagine that eventually I study music with learned teachers, well enough to hear the scores, follow the improvisations, and even dream of conducting something by Mahler. (I like the way the last movement of his 1896 Third Symphony inspired Sammy Fain's 1938 tune, "I'll Be Seeing You in Old Familiar Places.") I would hope to be able to love Mahler's Third in a deeper, broader way than now, and give it an intelligent interpretation. But I suspect my new understanding will be a development of my early, uninformed but enthralled understanding of this work, which first spoke to me very specifically. Best case: while the musical explanations I learn will be clarifying, my new, enriched understanding will be much more than my new, technical grasp of Mahler—and will be in some continuity with my early inspiration. Worst case: my interpretation of Mahler will be reductive, dull, and uninspiring—missing the emotion for the notes. But in either case, it will be Mahler's Third Symphony sounding, not my "theory of Mahler's Third."

One more musical note. Since the meaning, emotion, and sensation literally emerges in front of the score and the orchestra, not from behind them, you need to get yourself there, in front, for the music to wash over you and send you away dancing. So it is with the text, the preacher, and the congregation.

In the fourth chapter of Luke, the amazed people in the synagogue at first appear to understand Jesus's text from Isaiah, but then things go wrong. As if mistrusting their initial understanding, they seek explanations. They ask, "Is this not Joseph's son?" (4:22b). Notice, in this case, the question does not concern the message of Isaiah, nor even the message of Jesus, but of the ancestry of the messenger, with all the ambiguity that "Joseph's son" implies. Was the message of divine liberation lost on them? Not entirely, for they would have been familiar with Isaiah, and they were indeed amazed. But then they distracted themselves with the wrong sort of question—a reductive question—and things went bad from there. However, give those Nazarenes some credit for their amazement. They had made a good start.

To James Harris, then, the task of sermon preparation and preaching is to enrich one's initial amazement *and* one's initial uncertainty, never losing touch with the music and meaning of liberation. Harris calls upon the preacher and the congregation together to follow scriptural and

xvi

contemporary narratives of God's deliverance inwardly and outwardly, to where gracious meaning transforms the world pastorally and prophetically. With compassionate rage at injustice, and while praying with peaceable humor for human foibles in the pews, Harris deftly blends apparent opposites: interpretation theory with homiletic practice, Jonah with James Baldwin, Black liberation theology with "writing" on the ground (John 8)—where Jesus "un-reads" an oppressive text of stony righteousness. In an era where post-factual politicians are daily inverting reality and social media risks emptying language of truthful power, Harris brilliantly shows how encountering the preached word can again be dangerous to all "the powers."

Larry D. Bouchard
University of Virginia

PREFACE

The earliest permanent message from my first year of seminary was that the interpreter of the scripture should allow the text to speak for itself. James Henry Harris, in his latest push for homiletical excellence, has produced a masterful piece on the credibility of the text. Indeed, he embraces the idea that the text can, will, and must speak for itself. In this way, the text is not limited to one prescribed interpretation, but the text is set free to continue to offer new meaning. And, the reader of the text is liberated to discover more of what the text discloses. After teaching preaching for over twenty years, it is not unusual to hear students, colleagues, and others who have surveyed a text be delighted to find that the text can say more. Harris is suggesting that scripture's capacity to say more is predicated upon the ability of an individual to shift or adjust their eyes, i.e., their understanding. It is this shifting or adjusting of the eyes that is under exploration in this work. Harris teaches us how to develop the ability to shift the eyes. To do so, requires a preaching technique that Harris is calling "getting in front of the text." It is this process that helps the reader indulge in the newness of meaning. Therefore, preaching a text for the twentieth time can be as refreshing as the first time. For this reason, beginning preachers, seminarians, preachers who have been at it for a while would want to read and benefit this book.

Since the religious community has come under scrutiny, I find it commendable that Harris "thought it not robbery" to name a practice that has been embraced historically by members of the African American preaching community. Although, he formulates what he is calling "getting in front of the text," he is not claiming that this practice originates with him and this gives him credibility as a scholar, practitioner, teacher, and preacher. Harris should be applauded for the insight to prescribe a name for this practice, as well as get credit for doing the arduous work of un-veiling the peculiarities of this model. I appreciate his ability to develop a process that one can practice repeatedly. The way Harris frames his model eliminates guesswork and brings to the forefront for all to see and benefit from what it means to "get in front of the text." The application of this model is demonstrated throughout this work and proves to be a practical approach for successfully finding new insight. When the idea of "getting in front of the text" is placed under the microscope, it allows the reader to fully understand the model—what it offers —and how it might be used to explore preaching passages. This view of preaching could have been presented by the likes of Katie Geneva Cannon in *Teaching Preaching*, Cleophus James LaRue in *The Heart of Black Preaching*, Gennifer Brooks in *Good News Preaching* or Frank A. Thomas in *They Like to Never Quit Praisin' God*, but they did not. Therefore, Harris is the first to name it, and this highlights his high regard for the practice of preaching and undoubt-edly designates him as a premiere and cutting-edge homiletician. *Beyond the Tyranny of the Text* makes it clear that Harris is concerned about help-ing preachers. Those who have studied in seminaries and religious studies departments across the globe as well as those who have not walked the halls of academia will gain access to information that will help preaching regain its authority.

It is good to see in this work that Professor Harris has not vectored from the claim that preaching at its best is comprised of scholarship, a kind of learning that preachers from all walks of life can participate in on a personal level. Harris lays the groundwork to get preachers involved in the process of gleaning from the biblical text without being held hostage to systems that may preclude the unearthing of the gospel message that is inherently a part of every preaching text. I think preachers and homileti-cians like Samuel DeWitt Proctor, Gardner Taylor, Miles Jerome Jones, Ella Mitchell, Prathia Hall Wynn, and others would applaud Harris, as I do, for remaining faithful to keeping scholarship at the forefront of Black preaching. Therefore, this work becomes a critical resource for enhanc-ing the preaching message. Harris's model serves as a testament to itself;

it requires a reader's investment in "getting in front of the text." Even this book needs those who read it to "get in front of the text." Getting in front of the text is Harris's model/method for liberating the reader from a recurring deja vu experience while exploring familiar texts. The Harris model sets one up to see the biblical text afresh, anew, not "again." "Again," suggests something stale and stagnant in the mind of and view of the reader. "Again," conjures up old ideas and systems of authority that are used to pin the reader in such a way that nothing new ascends from the literature/reading. Harris does not ask the reader to abandon form or historical critical discussions, consultation with commentaries or counsel from other biblical studies resources, he asks the interpreter of the text to permit the text to speak for itself. To employ the Harris model unveils new and creative possibilities in interpretation. One will not be locked into a framework of definite rules of engagement that limit one's ability to enjoy infinite textual meaning. For Harris, "getting in front of the text" is more than acknowledging context, culture, and the world around the biblical characters. All of what the exegete knows before coming to this reading enhances understanding as Harris commends the constitutive elements of "getting in front of the text:" Reading, Re-reading, Writing, Un-writing, and Re-writing the text.

Harris's benevolence to those who grind in the work of homiletics invites all preachers to the table so that we can be inspired to preach sermons that reach and impact the listener. This book *Beyond the Tyranny of the Text* is breaking new ground for sure. The preaching playing field is leveled. All preachers are afforded equal footing. In the past, preaching has been relegated to two camps: Black and white or maybe even subgroups of females and males. The practice of "getting in front of the text" lends itself to becoming the great equalizer. No individual who embraces this practice is subject to the negatives that have been associated with preaching in the past. "Getting in front of the text," creates no hierarchy of meaning.

Moreover, race, ethnicity, and gender are no longer negatives. Whatever the exegete brings to the table becomes advantageous in seeing additional meaning in the text. This is exciting for the field of Homiletics! To allow ones' authentic self and one's condition of existence to inform the search for meaning changes how the text is interpreted. Preaching becomes personal, communal, and relevant for the preacher and the hearers. Preaching has now become opened up to all. As the floodgates of textual meanings open, the hearer has the opportunity to experience the life-giving power of the sermon. Now "getting in front of the text" infiltrates and influences preaching simultaneously. Harris declares that "getting in front of the text" is what Jesus does in the gospels. For example, when Jesus finishes his discussion with the woman caught in adultery it initially seems that she was destined to die at the hands of the rock throwers but Jesus re-interprets the Law in such a way that this hated woman gets to walk away because Jesus "gets in front of the text." Jesus's re-reading of the Law was with insight that did not result in a death sentence for the woman whom the text indicates was "caught in the very act" (John 8:4). Jesus himself was able to rescue the scripture from an old interpretation, a singular focus for understanding by shifting his eyes. When Jesus shifts his eyes, (re-interprets) the scripture that was quoted to trap or to find cause against Jesus is now used to liberate the woman. Jesus is now able to see something different, and moves from and old understanding to a new creative understanding. Therefore, when Harris talks about intentionally relinquishing methods that are delimiting to see something new in the text the reader gains access to meaning that had not been heretofore discovered. For me, it is exciting to know that what was once considered a mystery can now be identified. *Beyond the Tyranny of the Text* will move the reader from a dogmatic "this is what the text means" to a different meaning... it also means this. Our eyes (mind) are free to see the text, to shift, and to adjust... to "get in front of the text" where transformation and liberation reside.

Charlotte McSwine
Proctor School of Theology
Virginia Union University

ACKNOWLEDGMENTS

Preaching is first and foremost an act of love, and churches still privilege it every Saturday, Wednesday, and Sunday morning around the world. I am more than grateful to those who have provided me the opportunity to practice ministry for several decades now. My two pastorates—first at Mt. Pleasant Baptist Church in Norfolk, Virginia, and now at Second Baptist Church in Richmond, Virginia—have been a blessing and a challenge. Also, I am grateful to the many graduate students who have helped me to refine my ideas by registering for my classes year after year. They have often challenged me to be more precise and more compassionate in my teaching. My passion for teaching preaching comes from God, who is my strength.

There is, however, a big difference between preaching, teaching preaching, and writing about preaching. Because the written word is a bit more distant from the hearer and reader, I have to work hard at making sure that the flavor, tone, and tenor of my written language struggles to be commensurate with my spoken language. Preaching is basically oral and in the final analysis requires something more than what writing demands. Nevertheless, they both must be merged if the sermon is to transform lives.

Thanks to Larry Bouchard and Peter Ochs, who read and provided valuable feedback on the early drafts of this manuscript. These two compassionate professors have helped me in ways that have sharpened my understanding of phenomenology, theology, hermeneutics, ethics, culture, and the life of study—all of which I apply to preaching as an interdisciplinary discipline.

Thanks to Charlotte McSwine-Harris, Robert Wafawanaka, Yung

Suk Kim, Vanessa Jackson, and Boykin Sanders, who have offered some form of critique and assistance throughout the development of this book. Also, thanks to members of the Academy of Homiletics, where I have shared many of these ideas, most recently in the work group of Bible and hermeneutics.

I thank the Hampton Minister's Conference for inviting me to lecture on preaching, and I commend the president and the officers for selecting a very challenging yet encouraging theme: "Preaching Forward, Forward Preaching: Preaching for Transformation." The three key words are *preaching, forward*, and *transformation*, which provide us with an opportunity to build and create new horizons for the critically important task of preaching. Thanks to Dwight Riddick; Deborah Haggins, the Hampton University chaplain and also executive director and treasurer of the Hampton University Ministers Conference; and William Harvey, Hampton University president; and the thousands of ministers and pastors whose love and respect for preaching as a demonstration of the Holy Spirit. Both of my sons, James Corey and Cameron C. Harris, graduated from this esteemed university. My wife, Demetrius, and I had an eight-year run from 2000 to 2008 as parents of two Hampton University graduates.

Thanks to John W. Kinney, Corey D. B. Walker, and the faculty of The School of Theology at Virginia Union University, who allowed me to present some form of this book as the inaugural lecture upon being promoted to Distinguished Professor in Preaching during the 2016 Ellison-Jones Convocation. Thanks always to my lovely wife, Demetrius; my dedicated Second Baptist Church leaders, Gregory Turner Sr., Mary Hicks, Evelyn Price, Geraldine Lemon, John, Barbara, and Kim Allen, Henry and Joan Tucker, Eddie and Amanda Mobley, Margaret Robertson, Allen Robinson, Janith Libron, Alton Hart, James Jones, Bernie and MacDaniel Anderson, Clifford and Shirley Harris, Floyd Bradby, Antonio and Erica Redd, Myles Russell, JaRon Mathis, Marion Blackwell, Gloria Lucas, Lucy and Harry Jones, Sequan Crenshaw, Venessa and Daniel Bond, James and Alana Giles, Beverley Walker, Chris Stevens, Aaron and Brittney Dobynes, Beverley Epps, Pam Brown, Sylvanius Brown, Charis Harris, Cynthia Coles, and many others who filled in the gap as I spent countless hours in the library, preaching, and lecturing around the country. To anyone who played a part in helping this book come to fruition, I am forever grateful.

Thanks to Charles Gillespie for his creative, meticulous, and insightful suggestions, edits, and encouragement in the development of this book. Thanks to Jerome and Jeromyah Jones for their artistic rendering of the diagram in the front part of the book and to Douglas Harris who architecturally tweaked the diagram. Thanks also to Lisa Lawrence Wilson, Dwayne Whitehead Sr., Akeem Walker, Joshua Mitchell, Eric Gill, Melvin Cotton, Steve Parker, and David Jones for their encouragement and excitement about this book project and what it means for teachers of theology, ethics, homiletics, pastors, and the church. Thanks to Yohance D. Whitaker, Tony Baugh, Lisa Lawrence, and Lance Watson, Jr. for their work as my research assistants and pursuing excellence. Finally, thanks to Abingdon Press and their team of editors, especially Connie Stella and Laurie Vaughen.

The Black Baptist Church is my base and the context of my practice of theology and preaching. To all who love and support the church, I say "Praise God, thank you Jesus."

INTRODUCTION

Make an effort to present yourself to God as a tried-and-true worker, who doesn't need to be ashamed but is one who interprets the message of truth correctly.

—2 Timothy 2:15

There are those who believe that preachers, like other leaders, are born and not made. Robert J. McCracken, in the Lawrence Stone Lectures at Princeton given around the time I was born, said that preachers are born and not made.[1] But I say to you that preachers are made and not born! They are made through the hard and laborious work of study and praxis, the basic practices of interdisciplinary reading and writing sermons over and over again. They are made and shaped by the mind and Spirit.

There are those who possess what are often termed "natural gifts," such as height, complexion, skin tone, beauty, good looks, or voice (whether bass, baritone, alto, or soprano). These gifts are from God and heaven above by way of DNA, ancestry, and geography. Yes, there are those born with certain gifts or attributes, and while all of these aesthetic qualities are blessings and assets, they can also be curses and liabilities. I say this because those who are born with these attributes and qualities did not have to do anything to earn them and often do not do much of anything to develop them. That is the sin of giftedness because it tends to separate the gifted preacher from the God who blesses him or her. Certain skin tones and hair texture are natural attributes, and the preacher who possesses these often has an edge on those less endowed because the Black church is emotionally drawn to certain physical traits and characteristics that have little to nothing to do with intellectual ability, scholarship, spiritual

---

1. Robert J. McCracken, *The Making of a Sermon* (New York: Harper and Bros., 1956).

1

maturity, commitment, or any godly trait. It has only to do with the perceived aesthetic, the peripheral and ancillary attributes of being human. But even what appears ancillary may, in fact, be essential; and conversely, what appears to be essential may, in fact, be ancillary.

I am honored to stand on the shoulders of some of my mentors—Samuel DeWitt Proctor, Miles Jerome Jones, and others. Some of my students have encouraged me during the time I have been teaching preaching to one group or another, since I was twenty-four years old in the Norfolk extension of the Evans-Smith Institute, sponsored by Virginia Union University and the Baptist General Convention of Virginia. Some of these preachers and teachers have raised the bar for me and others before "crossing the bar" into the sunset of the promised land, in the language of Alfred Lord Tennyson, quoted so often by Black preachers.

Preaching is a spiritual, textual, and contextual enterprise that must be elaborated upon with newness and creativity. The preacher is always trying to find the spiritual wisdom and the language to inspire and encourage; to commend and correct; to cheer and chide where necessary, in the same spirit of 2 Timothy 4:2, which says, "Preach the word. Be ready to do it whether it is convenient or inconvenient. Correct, confront, and encourage with patience and instruction." My commitment is to help us together as preachers to become more diligent and inspired to always do our best in what I consider the most important calling on God's great earth—the preaching of the word of God.

I will explore this theme under the thesis and screen of "Getting in Front of the Text" as a new paradigm for preaching and sermon development. This language has been used by a few biblical scholars, exegetes, and philosophers. As preachers, we cannot do much transforming from behind. We have to get in front of the text if we want to preach forward or preach for transformation.

Some may ask, why this book? What is the motivation to write another book on preaching and interpretation? I decided to write this book because I wanted to move beyond traditional straitjacket exegesis to action, which is what philosopher Paul Ricoeur helps us do. He explains how to do interpretation and how to pivot toward getting in front of the text. But he doesn't really show us how to do this, which is a critical part of what I endeavor to do in this book. So, I have laid out a five-part method and theory for getting in front of the text that includes *reading, re-reading, un-reading, writing,* and *re-writing* (or the act of actually preaching the sermon).

I am fascinated with Ricoeur's theory of interpretation, which, after fifteen years of study, convinces me that preaching can benefit from his theoretical or phenomenological approach to interpretation and the nature of dialectics, especially event and meaning, distanciation and appropriation, and understanding and explanation. But, more particularly, I believe that interpretation theory can be appropriated to the practice of preaching because every sermon is an interpretation of a scripture text, which is itself an interpretation. There is no way to avoid or escape the process of interpretation in the development and delivery of sermonic discourse. And every utterance that pours forth faith from the mouth of the preacher is the result of interpreting the scripture text, the self, the social and congregational context, and the broader cultural context.

This book is also written to help bridge the ubiquitous gap that exists between theory and practice by providing a new way of approaching the scripture text in the development of the sermon. If Ricoeur is right, and I think that he is, then scripture text provides the preacher with the opportunity to speak freedom and liberation to a whole new generation of students, preachers, pastors, teachers, and congregants in a way that is restricted only by the limitations of one's reading and imagination. The ability to make the scripture text one's own and to allow the text to create a new world is nothing short of transformative, cataclysmic, and potentially revolutionary. Just as love is a revolution for Kierkegaard, preaching is a revolution for the Black Church and me.

In practice, getting in front of the text can help rescue preaching from the doldrums of past practices and ignite a flame of fire in the sermon that cannot be hidden or extinguished in the deep caves and crevices of the author's mind, no matter how sharp and progressive he or she may be. It is both the present and the future that the sermon seeks to rehabilitate and transform by its creative and disclosive power. The preacher gives voice to this creative and cataclysmic enterprise—a new voice never before heard from the pulpit or from the public square.

Again, this book is written to show why and how the preacher can benefit from understanding that theory is not an isolated symbolic structure that has no relationship with practice. Theory is practice, and practice is theory in action. Interpretation theory propels me to practice and to endeavor to figure out how to concretize in sermonic form what theoreticians like Ricoeur write about so eloquently (albeit densely).

The issue of race in America supersedes almost everything: rationality, enlightenment, baptism, confession of Christ, fairness, justice, education, ethics, theology, among other things. And in light of the confounding election of Donald Trump to our nation's highest office, I've revised Ricoeur's profound idiomatic expression "the symbol gives rise to thought" from his book *The Symbolism of Evil.* Ricoeur's expression is revised by me to: "the symbol gives rise to thoughtlessness."

I am caught in a vortex of anger, anxiety, paralysis, and despair. And yet I am not so angry that I am without hope or without the drive to keep pressing forward. I have always felt the sting of racism on a daily basis, and I have sought to call the demon by its name in my study, writings, and preaching. My prayer is that those who are in constant denial of the racism and white supremacist ideology that permeate the evangelical church in America and the world will recognize that the election of a misogynist billionaire and vulgar capitalist to the highest office in the free world is an affront to women, poor people, and democracy; it proves that democratic principles, the white church in America, and the evils of hatred and injustice have come together in unholy matrimony as a confluence of "family values" and white evangelicalism to "make America great again" after civil rights, minority rights, and the election of a Black president. The word "again" in the political slogan is a sign of white supremacy and a call to resist and turn back the clock regarding civil and human rights.

Method: How to Preach with Words

In an effort to ground this book in theory and practice and to advance both prophetic discourse and sermonic methodology, I am using the book of Jonah, an extraordinary narrative, to develop a short sermonic discourse to frame each chapter.

The book of Jonah is a short story or a novella that is unlike typical prophetic books. In the Christian canon, Jonah is one of the twelve minor prophetic books. The prophetic Book of the Twelve is a compilation or anthology of small books on one scroll in both the Hebrew Bible and the Qumran manuscripts. These books are bound by eschatological themes as reflected in the futuristic phrases "Day of the Lord" and "on that day." The eschatological focus of these books contributed to their inclusion at the end of the Christian canon, where they could point to the New Testament. That is, the prophecies of all the prophets were believed to be fulfilled in the coming of Jesus. That is why New Testament writers like Matthew cite the Old Testament to show the fulfillment of prophecy (cf. 1:22-23).

But in the Hebrew Bible, Jonah is considered one of the Writings (*Ketuvim*) and not one of the Prophets (*Nevi'im*). In the Hebrew Bible, prophetic books occupy the middle corpus between the Law/Torah and the Writings. As such, prophetic books added commentary to the Torah and its legal injunctions.[2]

In sum, the prophetic preacher Jonah is sent to preach to Nineveh, but his xenophobia leads him to get on a boat heading to Tarshish—which is in the opposite direction! While aboard the boat, a storm comes. By divination, the mariners figure out that Jonah is responsible for the storm, and Jonah is caught and thrown into the sea. He is swallowed by "a big fish" and is in its belly for three days before he says a prayer of repentance and is spat back upon the shore.

The story is full of literary elements of irony, hyperbole, exaggeration, and humor. For example, in folkloristic fashion, even the animals in Nineveh fast and are clothed in sackcloth; the city of Nineveh is described

---

2. See John J. Collins, *Introduction to the Hebrew Bible*, 2nd ed. (Minneapolis: Fortress, 2014), 437–41; and Michael D. Coogan, *The Old Testament: A Historical and Literary Introduction to the Hebrew Scriptures*, 2nd ed. (New York: Oxford University Press, 2011), 516–17. I am also grateful for the class notes from Old Testament Professor Robert Wafawanaka's Introduction to Biblical Studies course at Virginia Union University School of Theology, Richmond, Virginia, in the fall of 2015.

as requiring three days to traverse (perhaps three miles); Jonah is more concerned about the withered bush than about the Ninevites, and Jonah is hurt when the Ninevites repent (showing his lack of compassion). The book has both a contextual and universalistic outlook and inclusive appeal. Yahweh is not just concerned about Israel alone, but also about the Ninevites and their well-being. The Ninevites, and their animals, can be saved and worship Yahweh, even though Israel's prophet is disobedient, hardheaded, and xenophobic. The universal message of the book of Jonah may be in contradistinction to the exclusive approaches of Ezra and Nehemiah in the postexilic period. Both of those prophets were wrestling with the results of cultural mixing and mixed marriages (such as Solomon's).

Go for Substance with Style

It is important for the preacher to realize that the sermon must not be boring. At all cost, the Black preacher must know that boredom in preaching is a cardinal sin, or what Fred Craddock called "the demon." This means that substance and style are the twin engines that drive the sermon and keep it moving forward. There is no necessary opposition between the two; substance and style help each other like *what* and *how*. I can relate this to a doctor who has spent many years in the classroom studying the *what* of medicine and likewise has spent an equal number of years in clinic, residency, and fellowships practicing the *how* of medical procedures. There is no licensed doctor who does not know both *what* to do and *how* to do it. One of these gifts without the other is almost useless.

And, this is the expectation of those to whom I teach preaching and those in my congregation who listen to and hear preaching Sunday after Sunday. In both the classroom and the pulpit, there is a noble need to know what and how to preach, how to put the sermon together, and how to keep the congregation from becoming bored with the sermon. It is a fallacy and a fiction to think that content and style, or matter and manner, can be separated without serious and devastating consequences that lead ultimately to the death of the sermon and the death of the church. Style is content, and content is style, to paraphrase Friedrich Nietzsche on the one hand and the historical Black preacher on the other hand.[3] The Black preacher's often hyperbolic stylistics can potentially mediate against content.

Nevertheless, I am acutely aware that stylistics is an art form in the Black church and absolutely integral to effective preaching, although it is often frowned upon by whites who generally think that anything that Black people do is anemic until they put their *imprimatur* on it. This is a form of stealing or hijacking an art form developed and practiced by the Black preacher who, according to W. E. B. Du Bois, was a "boss" and master of this type of sermonic performance culminating in a Black church "frenzy."

Today, more and more white preachers are beginning to realize that their "straitjacket" approach to pulpit and pew is contributing to the death of the white mainline protestant church. To counter this reality and the impending doom of their seeming hatred of emotions evidenced by foregrounding cognition and creating an unnecessary dichotomy between style and substance, they have begun to reluctantly embrace the intuitive, rhythmic cadences, teachings, and practices of the Black preacher and the Black church. We see this in jazz programs all over the nation, where the music of Black Africa and America has been commandeered by whites.

This is not unique to music and has also been seen in many other fields. African Americans are picking up on how this clandestine practice of robbery is taking place. In the words of Jesse Williams,

We're done watching and waiting while this invention called whiteness uses and abuses us, burying black people out of sight and out of mind while extracting our culture, our dollars, our entertainment like oil—black gold—ghettoizing and demeaning our creations then stealing them, gentrifying our genius and then trying us on like costumes before discarding our bodies like rinds of strange fruit.... Just because we're magic doesn't mean we're not real.[4]

---

3. See for example, Friedrich Nietzsche, *The Birth of Tragedy* (Cambridge: Cambridge University Press, 1999), and Martha Nussbaum, *Love's Knowledge* (New York: Oxford University Press, 1990).

4. Megan Lasher, "Read the Full Transcript of Jesse Williams' Powerful Speech on Race at the BET Awards," *Time*, June 27, 2016, http://time.com/4383516/jesse-williams-bet-speech-transcript/.

Hence, white preachers and teachers are taking a more serious look at what they can learn, borrow, and steal from the Black preacher and the Black church, which at its core, regardless of denomination, is in fact quite "Pentecostal." By this I mean expressive, celebrative, spiritual, and unrestrained by the right side of the brain, creating a balance and holistic approach to preaching and worship. Preaching is both a cognitive and emotive enterprise, especially in the Black church tradition.

The Method: Reading as an Act of Love in the Dialectic of Practice

Reading is the first step in this process, and such reading is a "close reading" of the text. This means that the preacher reads the text with whatever facility he or she brings to the scripture. There are no perfect readers. For a few people, this facility will include languages of multiple origins, and for others, it will be their seeking to master their native tongue. Either way, I perceive close reading as an interdisciplinary process that demands a macrocosmic understanding of getting at textual meaning through an expanded reading program that includes a regular regimen of novels of all stripes and colors, as well as history, philosophy, theology, poetry, and sermons (published and unpublished, written, and spoken).

This also includes listening to music of all genres: jazz, R&B, country, classical, hip-hop, rap, and so on. Music is a language of love and spirit and helps to ground and focus our understanding beyond the use of words. Music and musicality are necessary to the actual preaching of the sermon, and the sermon is a musical score that traverses the scale of flats and sharps, highs and lows, melody and harmony. The sermon, when rightly done, sings to the glory of God. After developing this broad-based reading and listening skill, then there is a need to have a microcosmic approach to the text as well, honing in on the specifics of the chosen text like a mountain lion devouring its prey—or more like enjoying its feast. This "feasting on the word" is at its core a reading and studying project. Read the chosen text to the point of minimal understanding or a first understanding, which will demand a close re-reading. Re-reading is an ongoing process that must be developed.

Re-reading as an Act of Faith in the Dialectic of Practice

Re-reading never ends because we seldom fully reach the point of an ultimate reading. The weakness of the written text is in its ability to quell conversation and to mute interrogation of its claims, pretending to be authoritative and seeking to mask its hegemonic arrogance and violence. Thus, an ultimate reading of a text brings silence and death to the text and practices a violence that I both shun and deplore. So re-reading is a continuous endeavor or process that can be done daily as a way of seeking to integrate the text into the preacher's pores, into his or her consciousness as a way of remembering and reflecting. Re-reading is key to this process and method of getting in front of the text in order to understand and interpret the text.

Un-reading as an Act of Re-understanding and Appropriation

Un-reading the text is the third and critical step in this five-part method for preaching. To un-read is the beginning, or more precisely, the renewal of interpretation. Un-reading is the act of reconfiguring the text in a way that is contextually relevant and pragmatic. It is the commitment to re-contextualize and appropriate the text to the current life situation of the community of free and oppressed people. In order for the preacher to advance understanding and the practice of freedom in the interpretation process, she must begin to un-read the text in an effort to allow the meaning of the text to perform its ability to transform and liberate the preacher and the congregation.

Un-reading can only be done after an extensive and close reading and re-reading. We, as preachers, *read* to *un-read*, which is to say that we read in order to put that reading in our own words, that is, to express our deep

9

understanding and not allow what others have written or said to bind and shackle us to the past or the present. Rather, we read to un-read in order to free us to think new and transformative thoughts, which is the stuff of interpretation. Un-reading is a visionary and prophetic enterprise, a proleptic vision for the existing text and a new wording of the read and the re-read text.

Un-reading involves the first two steps in the process or method as a prelude and prolegomenon to the actual practice of un-reading, which is the fulcrum of this five-step method. Reading and re-reading for textual clues that suggest oppressive and hegemonic influences that demand challenge and confrontation means, for example, that any biblical text that lauds or even suggests that there is some virtue or ethical value in slavery or the dehumanization of the other demands an un-reading that recognizes the evils of slavery and injustice in any form. This also includes not only slavery, but other sinful acts of oppression and immorality.

All slavery is evil, no matter what spin the European exegetes and beneficiaries put on it. Many texts such as "Slaves, obey your masters..." (Col 3:22; cf. Eph 6:5 and 1 Pet 2:18-20) have to be acknowledged as colonialist, patriarchal, and evil. And this means that these texts, as well as those whose language is more subtle and nuanced, demand an *un-reading* by Black and white preachers and teachers. Dealing with Greek and Hebrew languages and explaining the history and theology behind the linguistics serve an admirable purpose; however, the word *slave* is offensive and oppressive, and no amount of explanation regarding its etymology or modern meaning in scripture can erase the anamnestic and terroristic feeling I have in encountering the word *slave* or any of its derivatives. They all point to a type of evil that rivals the demonic.

Un-reading requires a level of consciousness and boldness that few preachers can claim and name. It is to face head on the centuries of polemics embedded in the intertextuality of scripture, theology, and social theory—all encumbered by a "universalism" that is no more than localized hegemony masquerading as a globalized form of correct interpretation. This is the subtle nature of the banality of unfairness and evil that engulfs the church and society.

Un-reading as a concept and practice is the linchpin of this methodology. It is the central element, the essential pivot upon which the method hangs or revolves. It is in the middle, between reading and re-reading and writing and re-writing/preaching. This un-reading is the locus of freedom and transformation. The text is read in order that it can be *un-read*. Reading to un-read is the crux of prophetic and transformative preaching, as well as any preaching that seeks to address the social ills and economic disparities in our society. Un-reading is unbound by the intention of the author or the text itself. It is a radical vector toward freedom and a necessary prerequisite for writing and re-writing the sermon.

English professor John Guillory helps to provide clarity to this concept. He writes,

> The text that was thought to be comprehended remains still to be understood. Only at this point, in which reading reverses itself, in which the text at hand becomes suddenly unfamiliar and strange, does interpretation begin. Only when the longtime reader can say "I don't yet know how to read" or "I don't know how to read this text," does it become possible to make the conceptual break. [...] By *interpretation* I mean the capacity of a reader to re-understand the words of a text by translating those words into a new frame of reference or intelligibility.[5]

Interpretation and application go together. This is not even radical; it is traditional beginning with Augustine and continuing through Gadamer. So, there we have it! To un-read a text is to re-understand the text in a way that has not yet been comprehended or understood. This is to interpret and re-interpret the text, which is the necessary precondition to understanding the text for preaching the yet-unwritten sermon. And, as I tell my students, the sermon must be written because the writing of the sermon is an act of freedom for those who have been and continue to be oppressed. Writing is an act of subversive independence and creativity. Writing the sermon is the next step in this methodology.

---

5. John Guillory, "On the Presumption of Knowing How to Read," *ADE Bulletin* 145 (Spring 2008): 9.

Writing as Reflective Transformative Thinking

The fourth step in the process or method of getting in front of the text is writing. Writing takes place only after the preacher has been able to read, re-read, and un-read the text. This means that the process of writing can be quite unstructured at this point, in the sense that the focus is on understanding and interpreting the text based on the following factors:

A clear understanding of the wording, punctuation, and language of the text

How the text relates to the preacher's context and the broader social context

What the un-reading of the text has revealed that fosters liberation and transformation in the lives of the congregants to whom the sermon is addressed

It is important to know that this writing is a first writing, or first draft, that allows for misunderstanding and misinterpretation, which are normative elements in any process of understanding. Understanding, then, is a byproduct of misunderstanding, similar to Dietrich Bonhoeffer's notion of community as the coming to grips with illusion and disillusionment. Writing begins only when reading has been exhausted or partially exhausted, because there is no ultimately exhaustive reading. The exhaustion is in the reader of the text, not the text itself. However, in this sense, reading never ends, but the preacher must endeavor to write at some point, and that can only be determined by the individual reader and preacher.

This writing is not in outline form or note-taking but is sentential and discursive to the point of semantic excess. This excess will serve the preacher well when the fifth step in this process begins: re-writing.

Re-writing as Preaching the Sermon

Re-writing is the fifth and quasi-final stage of the methodology, which includes a more substantive architectonic or structure. By this, I mean

12

that the preacher can now decide how to apply all of his or her reading, re-reading, un-reading, and writing to the organization of the sermon, either as a dialectic, correlational, expository, or narrative type. The typology at this point becomes a way to develop plainly the direction or angle of the sermonic discourse. This methodology is superimposed on any of the above sermon structures because it is a prelude to structure. It is foundational.

Re-writing is also a streamlining of the first writing, extirpating all unnecessary wordiness and "fluff" in order to make the sermon fit and lean. This is hard for the preacher because many often feel that their words are invaluable and what they have written is something that must be said. However, it is the excising of words and phrases that leaves room for what in Black religion is often referred to as the "Holy Spirit's entrance into the sermon and into human affairs." This entrance of the Holy Spirit is an act of love that makes preaching possible.

Preaching is the knowledge and practice of agape love. This is often coupled with the dialogical nature of Black preaching and the congregation's participation in this process. Sometimes, this re-writing is an on-the-spot enterprise that is a result of the hearer's identification and verbalized support of the sermon. Expressed phrases as "Amen," "Say it, Preacher," or "Hallelujah" will serve to allow the sermon room to fill in some of the natural gaps in the sermonic text. At other times, the preacher will solicit witnesses to the proclaimed word when he or she feels that it is warranted or even unwarranted. In the Black church, the preacher will sometimes ask, "Can I get an Amen?" This shall be discussed and demonstrated in chapter five.

READING

Preaching for Transformation

Getting in Front of the Text: Metaphor and Metonymy

Getting in front of the text means reading the text according to what one sees and what one hears the text saying today. It is a quest for a new understanding based on context. It is a cultural hermeneutical move that allows for the preacher to develop and maintain contiguity to the people in the church and the local community. Getting in front of the text is to understand the text in a way that creates proximity between the text and the people. In reading, one has to encounter the biblical world, the modern and postmodern world, and the world of the preacher and hearer. Getting in front of the text is both a rational and an emotive enterprise because they are "two sides of the same coin"—to speak both metaphorically and metonymically. There is both proximity and contiguity because both sides are needed in order to have something we call a "coin."

Each generation has to read the text in an effort to get in front of it, i.e., to make it relevant for today and tomorrow. Any preaching that does not get in front of the text is probably irrelevant because getting behind the text has no ultimate meaning for today's social and political challenges. In this sense, getting in front of the text is a social and contextual move designed to create new horizons and a new world absent of oppression and injustice.

Since one cannot readily, literally get in front of a text, a grouping of words in a logical order connected by typology across bound sheets of paper, there is a figurative element to the homology of orienting and positioning oneself with regard to a text that is not in the physical arena but in the spiritual and cognitive. Now, it is true that a person can stand literally in front of a text. A book. Great. But what good does this do a person's psyche? Beyond looking odd behaviorally, how does this geographic, topographic alteration of space inform a person's sensibility and understanding? It does in the same way that rubbing or embracing an oak tree speaks to our fragility, finiteness, and other elements spatially and self-consciously. Getting in front of a text is not simply about standing before a tome awaiting it to pour out its logics and musics and universes of discourse into your social imagination. It is about cultivating an understanding of the text that lends itself to the text being alive, being fallible, being useless, being instrumental, being redemptive, being generative, and being transformative. This being of the text, the imbuing the text with its own historical and existential force, allows its interlocutors to orient themselves with it in such a way as to remain behind the meanings of each phoneme rendered as immortal thought. This being of the text allows us to place oneself at the ungodly mercy of the author's intention, or posturing oneself in a hermeneutic of the yet unexplored eternal weight of what the text promises to do. Futurity is in this metaphorical way of looking at text. One can and should literally and metaphorically get in front of the text.

With metonymy this matter of orientation to text does not only relate to a cognitive quality that becomes an existential imperative but its natural motility is towards contiguity. This contiguity can be literal, which may grant it a different set of significations (for example: living in a literal country having literal laws, textually prescribed, intellectually internalized), or it may have a figurative character, that may yield a hermeneutic refinement instructive for a more purposive and prophetic interpretation. If we keep the same cognitive orientation towards the text explored in the metaphorical function of the phrase "getting in front of the text," we can add the metonymic function now that we are in front, by positing these questions: How do we touch the text? How do we allow the text to touch us? How is our mental spatiality refined towards touching, handling the matter of a particular text? This is the essence of the proximity and contiguity of which I write. As the crown is a metonym for the Queen of England, touching her head, she being the monarchical ruler of a nation and its colonies, the interlocutor's metonymic orientation to text can be qualified with comparable metrics. How does the text touch the interlocutor's imagination? Is it a linguistic haptics that ascend weakness and looks at the text from a position of power; is it a touching that orients the reader towards an empathy for marginalized groups and oppressed peoples? This is the metonymic quality of getting in front of the text, thus, my aphoristic statement: "getting in front of the text is metaphoric and metonymic."

More precisely, getting in front of the text is metaphoric because it signifies an explosion of meaning and hope. This figurative explosion, or more plainly, the new information disclosed when getting in front of the text, finds its place in the "live" metaphoric references of Interpretation Theory. This pivotal, liberative notion, as Ricoeur concurs, seeks to tell us something new about reality.[1] Ricoeur lends a rhetorical treatment to the "live" metaphor, wherein he construes it to be semantic innovation that supplies a new extension of meaning.[2] It is a strategic, and even an unexpected arrangement of words that convey a new thought or explanation. Unlike "dead" metaphors, such as "the foot of a chair," that pervade our discourse in ordinary circulation, "live" metaphors are new entries and contributors to our polysemic system that have the potential to jolt our understanding of the world. Just as "dead of night" conveys the stillness or silence of the night and an "ocean of tears" gives rise to the act of weeping heavily; all metaphors move beyond lexical code and enter the phenomenon of rhetoric to resolve the occurrences of reality. Getting in

---

1. Paul Ricoeur, *Interpretation Theory: Discourse and Surplus of Meaning* (Fort Worth: Texas Christian University Press, 1976), 53.

2. Ricoeur, *Interpretation Theory*, 52.

front of the text moves beyond the static parameters of biblical interpretation and into the explosion of meaning and hope of the biblical text for life as it is today.

Getting in front of the text is also a metonym for liberation. As an action, it presents itself in close proximity to the oppressed. This symbolic phrase calls forward the subversive acts of Jesus of Nazareth as he spoke against the oppressive structures of his time. Getting in front of the text is an act of freedom that equates to and is the trope of liberation because it counters oppressive interpretations of the bible. Not discounting historical criticism from its Eurocentric preoccupation with getting behind the text to seek understanding of the author's intent at the time it was written, but rather getting in front of the text begins with the present possibility of hope for today, while creating the way for bringing about a new world.

JONAH I: "The Unwelcomed Word"

> *Now the word of the LORD came to Jonah son of Amittai, saying,*
> *"Go at once to Nineveh, that great city,*
> *and cry out against (her) it; for their wickedness has come up before me."*
> *But Jonah set out to flee to Tarshish from the presence of the LORD.*
> *He went down to Joppa and found a ship going to Tarshish;*
> *so he paid his fare and went on board, to go with them to Tarshish,*
> *away from the presence of the LORD.*

—Jonah 1:1-3 (NRSV)

To welcome one another is the essence of hospitality. It seems that we are excited and welcoming of almost anything and everybody. We love to welcome so much that it is not unusual for us to throw a party, do a dance, bring out the champagne or the Bud Light—you name it and we can show our excitement in celebrating a birthday, promotion, retirement, or graduation. We welcome these events with open arms and a joyous spirit. And sometimes we act so crazy that the neighbors have to call the police, especially after incidents of police brutality like the events at Ferguson.

But I tell you, Black people need to be leery and careful about calling the police. Try not to call them for anything because as a Black person, you could end up dead, killed by the police that you thought naively were going to help you. The law and those enforcing the law have never been on the side of Black people. In New York in 2014, the police ganged up on Eric Garner put him in a chokehold, beat, kicked, and pounded his head against the concrete sidewalk while the man was yelling that he couldn't breathe. The paramedics were just as bad by spectating rather than resuscitating. This is criminal. This is legalized criminality. If you are Black, it may be a sign of our having good sense *not* to get involved with the police. These are the folk that you need to flee from. And this is some of what should be unwelcomed, but not only that. We are so ungodly in our attitudes and actions.

We welcome everything and everybody except the word and presence of the Lord. Jonah's spirit lives in each of us. God tells us to do one thing and we do another. God says go this way and we go another way. "The word of the Lord came to Jonah son of Amittai saying, 'Go at once to Nineveh . . . and cry out against it; for their wickedness has come up before me.'" Jonah is asked to preach against wickedness, to speak out against all the evil and ugliness. And he could not do it.

The word of the Lord was direct and to the point: Go to Nineveh and cry out against it. And the word of the Lord was unwelcomed. Jonah, like everyone else, was aware of the sins and wickedness of Nineveh, yet he could not do what God told him to do. It's not an easy task to preach hard truths to people who think they are great, and Nineveh was known as "a great city." We think that God has made a mistake and couldn't possibly be asking us to do that. But that's the meaning and nature of prophecy and prophetic preaching. Sometimes that's what has to be "did."

Cry out against sin and evil. Cry out against all the selling and use of drugs in the Black community. Cry out against oppression and hate, against lying and deceit, against greed and self-interest. Cry out against racism and injustice, against government power brokers. Cry out against practices in the church that are as wicked as practices in the world.

Getting in Front of the Text

The sense of the text is not behind the text, but in front of it.
It is not something hidden, but something disclosed.

—Paul Ricoeur

Everyone had always said that John would be a preacher when he grew up,
just like his father. It had been said so often that John, without ever thinking
about it, had come to believe it himself.

—James Baldwin, *Go Tell It on the Mountain*

Preaching is highly grounded in orality and I hasten to add that preaching benefits from repetition. I am interpreting "Preaching Forward—Preaching for Transformation" to mean "Getting in Front of the Text," which is an interpretation of what French philosopher Paul Ricoeur seeks to explain in his unique and insightful theoretical approach regarding texts. Yet, it is not so complicated that we can't understand its theory.

Not only do we seek to understand getting in front of the text, but in some strange and fruitful way, we tend to practice it, even if unknowingly. What I mean here is that Black preaching has historically practiced some form of this methodology as a way of negotiating scripture texts that were more than distant from and foreign to their lived experience. In other words, getting in front of the text was the only choice Black people had, because getting behind the text offered no freedom and very little hope. Pragmatism rules in Black religion and the Black church. So "we been doing" that for which we did not have a name.

We just did not name it. Nevertheless, I hope to present a type of unraveling of this perceived denseness and bring some semblance of clarity and plain sense to our understanding of the interpretation and preaching process because the preacher is always interpreting every time she or he writes and speaks the sermon.

The idea of getting in front of the text is a radical departure from what we have often been taught in colleges and seminaries about the meaning of scripture and the understanding of texts. The focus, historically, has been on getting behind the text. We dig up the archeological bones of the text or seek to find out what the text means today by trying to understand what it meant in the past, what it meant to the author and the long-dead ancient community to which it was addressed. We ask questions like: What was the original meaning of the scripture text? What does the historical-critical method have to say? What does the Greek or Hebrew language say and mean? Who was it written to, and why was it written in the first place?

I will be the first to admit that such reasoning has some meaning and value, but it is not crucial to anything regarding the transformation of the self and society today, right here and right now. Getting behind the text is a secondary action. As a matter of fact, doing this first could potentially cause your interpretation to be oppressive, restrictive, stultifying, and hopelessly romantic, similar to the reasoning of those in the legal field, who often claim to interpret the US Constitution by focusing on what the Founding Fathers "meant" or "intended" by their use of certain language.

But in my view, a very activist language promoting "state's rights" and other language essentially guaranteed slavery, women's disenfranchisement, and other forms of inequality and evil. No! I am not too interested in or impressed by what the text meant to the Hebrews, the Corinthians, the Ephesians, or to the churches of Asia Minor. I am very keenly interested, however, in what the text means today—right here and right now—to oppressive, oppressed, and poor people, to Black people, to young people, and to women and men struggling for peace, love, and justice.

So I'm telling you "from the jump" that this book is not going to talk about "getting behind the text," about biblical history and the intention of the author who wrote it. Who is to say that the authors, whoever they were, even knew what they meant when they wrote the text? I am surely not going to spend any time trying to find out myself about what somebody else meant or what their intention was when intention is so difficult and almost impossible to determine especially when the author of the text is dead. I believe that Ricoeur is right to suggest that the meaning of the text surpasses the intention of the author and the intention of the text itself. This book is about what it means to claim and to assert that the meaning of the text is *in front of it!* Not behind it! Ricoeur encourages us when he asserts the following in poetic, even oratorical style:

Not the intention of the author, which is supposed to be hidden behind the text; not the historical situation common to the author and his original readers; not even their understanding of themselves. . . . What has to be appropriated is the meaning of the text itself, conceived in a dynamic way as the direction of thought opened up by the text. In other words, what has to be appropriated is nothing other than the power of disclosing a world that constitutes the reference of the text. . . . If we may be said to coincide with anything it is not the inner life of another ego, but the disclosure of a possible way of looking at things, which is the genuine referential power of the text.[3]

Ricoeur sounds here like T. S. Eliot, who writes in *Four Quartets*,

Not the intense moment
Isolated, with no before and after,
But a lifetime burning in every moment
And not the lifetime of one man only
But of old stones that cannot be deciphered.[4]

The meaning of the text is the most important thing, even if we are guessing at it. In my view, the preacher's divine grammatical guessing at the meaning of the text for poor people, Black people, people who are hungry, and people who are oppressed is the first important step toward understanding the meaning of the text for the church and the community today. Meaning is textual and contextual. Even the slaves knew in their souls that the slave master had intentionally or unintentionally misinterpreted, misunderstood, and misrepresented the meaning of the biblical text. "Everybody talking about heaven ain't going there," they said as a response to the distanciation between the words of scripture and the actions of the slave master.

The meaning of the text itself is independent of the author's intention, if only because there is always a surplus of meaning outside of the author's

3. Paul Ricoeur, *Interpretation Theory: Discourse and Surplus of Meaning* (Fort Worth: Texas Christian University Press, 1976), 2. My understanding of Paul Ricoeur is best facilitated by the in-class lectures of Larry Bouchard, Professor at University of Virginia. See also David M. Rasmussen, *Mystic-Symbolic Language and Philosophic Anthropology* (Hague, Netherlands: Martinus Nijhoff, 1971).

4. T. S. Eliot, *Four Quartets* (New York: Harcourt, 1943), 31.

purview. The meaning of the text itself is independent from all external encumbrances, apart from the person doing the reading, re-reading, un-reading, writing, re-writing, and preaching. The text gives us clues as to what the author might have meant. The meaning of the text itself is found then in the text itself.

For those of us who study philosophical hermeneutics and biblical exegesis, there is an implicit understanding that text always means more than the author intended or meant to say. This is the "surplus of mean-ing." In the feel and the spirit of the text, meaning rises up and reveals itself in the soul and mind and heart of the text itself. Not outside, not underneath, not behind the text, but *in* the text. In the disclosive nature of the text resides the possibility of a new world—a world that we have never seen or experienced. It is not the world of the text, but the world that the text opens up for us. This world is a new entity created by the referential power of the text. This means that the future of the text is trans-formative—unfolding in ways not previously imagined by the writer or the previous readers. This is liberative. The text and its semantic autonomy harbor the creative power of the word of God and the wisdom of God.

This does not mean that the text is an isolated sage independent of all external wisdom. No, it waits anxiously for the poet (I mean the preacher) to mine its words for meaning, for a transforming interpretation so that it will not join the author as a dead entity. It waits with anticipation for the preacher to pay attention to every nuance found buried deep in its gram-mar, syntax, words, language, metaphors, and symbols. It waits in regal muteness, like a tall oak tree reaching toward heaven, just waiting for the voice of the preacher to transform its silence into a booming, transfor-mative chorus—a certain sound that has never been heard before by the writer or the historic interpreter of the text.

The scripture text is crying out, screaming and yelling for the preacher *not* to misinterpret its semiotics, its searing signs of redemption and hope. The text is waiting for the preacher to interpret and not misinterpret its language and its spirit—a Holy Spirit infused by the redemptive, powerful love of God and calling forth for a cataclysmic transformation and change of both individuals and society, speaking for love and justice and against hatred and evil. The scripture text is always trying to speak freedom and liberation for itself and the larger world, if the preacher will allow it, by freeing the text from its restless tides and from the binding hegemonies and political wrangling that continue to shackle it. The preacher and the church are as guilty as the rest of the world in trying to make everyone preach, look, smell, and sound the same! There is no forward moving transformation in sermons that sound alike. These are sermons that sound worn-over and worn-out, like stale bread and stagnant water.

Getting in front of the text allows the text to whisper, scream, and holler new meanings to the preacher as he or she listens to the revealing voice of the text and dares to preach with boldness, newness, contextual clarity, and unmatched understanding and faith—what the Greeks called "the divine madness."[5] With this faith, this divine madness, let your sermons call forth justice and righteousness. With this faith, this divine madness, let your preaching rise up from the manacles and shackles behind the text and get in front of the text, which is the only way for it to make a difference in a world that fears and resists change and transformation, a world that destroys the other in an effort to create sameness and stamp out difference.

Getting in Front of the Text: Possible Worlds

Preaching is an action, bold and often dangerous, and this action is itself a "text." Getting in front of the scripture text is a major part of the action I am talking about. It not only "projects a possible world,"[6] as Ricoeur asserts, but action also has a good chance of creating a world that serves as an alternative to the existing one. For example, I can imagine Rosa Parks rising up and going to the front seat of the bus in Montgomery, Alabama, in 1955. This action of "getting in front" is not simply metaphoric but metonymic—almost literal. The action that I am referring to requires a

---

5. See the introduction to Søren Kierkegaard's *Fear and Trembling and the Sickness Unto Death*, trans. Walter Lowrie (Garden City, NY: Doubleday, 1954), 10.

6. Ricoeur, *Interpretation Theory*, 87–88.

certain movement on the part of the preacher. The intention of the author may in fact be relevant and important, but it is not decisive.[7] The idea that the text creates a "possible world" is critical here because human possibility is the crux of freedom and transformation.

Conscientious and prophetic Black preachers and laypeople seemed to have believed this long before scholars like Ricoeur put it into words. The slaves, for example, saw possibility and a hope that prevented their extinction and made a way for freedom. Freedom is always only a possibility for the oppressed, and "freedom has always been an expensive thing," as Martin Luther King Jr. reminds us.[8]

Black liberation preaching and theology is all about creating and disclosing a possible world. Now, by getting in front of the text, I mean approaching the text by going through the front door of the scripture text, that is, finding a new contemporary point of entry. The act of getting in front of the text itself is grounded in having a hope and vision for the text that not even the past can control and the text itself cannot predict. To be sure, the text can explode with new meaning and hope, which is a powerful metaphor, but it is also a metonym, meaning that getting in front of the text depends on not being mesmerized by the past history of the text but being transformed by its eschatological future! A future pregnant with possibilities and hope.

It is what the text means now, today, in your context and congregation, that matters most. It is what the text says now that is important, not the finite horizon of the text's author that determines the contemporary meaning of the text. That is up to the intellectual creativity of the preacher. We have to extend the career of the text by getting in front of it every time we get a chance to use it as a foundation for the sermon— breaking it away from the tight grip of authority claimed by its author,

---

7. See Paul Ricoeur, *Hermeneutics and the Human Sciences* (Cambridge: Cambridge University Press, 1981), 15–16. And also John B. Thompson, *Critical Hermeneutics: A Study in the Thought of Paul Ricoeur and Jurgen Habermas* (Cambridge: Cambridge University Press, 1981). Thompson points out the gaps in Ricoeur's claim regarding reference and states, "How a text may disclose a possible world is quite unclear and how one may determine just which world it does disclose remains uncertain" (193).

8. Martin Luther King Jr., *The Essential Martin Luther King Jr.: 'I Have a Dream' and Other Great Writings* (Boston: Beacon, 2013), 33.

who no longer has any real practical authority on the text. The text has a new interpretation now, a new meaning that the preacher has given it by getting in front of it.[9]

As a Black preacher in America, reading is a critical act of freedom. For example, I am a part of a tradition that includes the evil experience of chattel slavery where learning to read in the English language was forbidden and punishable by death. I can still feel some semblance of its effects languishing in my collected subconscious. This is not my exclusive story because my own personal history and the history of others also help to constitute this tradition. I cannot escape the historical experience of the past—a past deeply rooted in suffering and highly correlated with the excess of evil perpetuated against a people whose only crime was the color of their skin. Reading is key to staying connected to past history and escape its debilitating effects when necessary.

Now this is where history and distanciation are incommensurate. There is no aesthetic or spiritual distance between slavery and myself, in the sense that every day I see in my mind's eye the bruising evils of slavery as I walk down the pathways of the James River and drive down Route 460 through Prince George, Sussex, Waverly, and Ivor, into the vicinity of Franklin and Southampton County, Virginia, where slave preacher Nat Turner died at the hands of the architects of the slavocracy. I can hear the echo of the Marabai, the echo of bloodhounds chasing the Black body. And I can see in my mind's eye the fear and the pain in the eyes of the slave women and men as they faced the despotic and demonic sovereign power of the evil slave master.

These haunting memories are instantiated in my being and mitigate against distanciation. This anamnesis is a recurring mimesis for me. What I mean here, is that memory continues to repeat or represent itself over and over again. Yes, there is clearly some space of time and place between then and now, but this is a past that is not dead for me. It is a sublation of death. This suffering survives the sting of death. It is "not even past," as William Faulkner says, because it haunts me and boggles my mind and spirit every

9. See Paul Ricoeur, "The Model of the Text: Meaningful Action Considered as a Text," *Journal of Social Research* 38, no. 3 (Fall 1971): 534.

single day. This is a type of torture that never escapes the Black conscious mind and body. This is the dilemma and crisis of the Black preacher in particular, and the conscious preacher in general.

Reading the Text

As a preacher, before you do anything else, you begin the sermon preparation process by choosing and settling on a scripture text. If you can read, then you can preach, but you have to have a text. No scripture text means no sermon. You may have a form of written discourse, but it is not even headed in the direction of a sermon. The text precedes a topic or title of a sermon. The title of the sermon grows out of the scripture text, not the other way around. So, choose the text first! You do this by reading and studying a little every day—not in search of something to preach but in search of feeding your soul, mind, and spirit. This approach will keep you from scrambling on Saturday and, God forbid, trying to get a sermon together on Sunday morning! The sermon needs time to marinate and seep into the pores of your body and soul. And it needs prayer, which should be an integral part of reading.

After settling on a scripture text for the foundation of the sermon, I recommend reading the chosen text in at least five different English translations such as the New Revised Standard Version (NRSV), the New International Version (NIV), the Good News Bible, the King James or New King James Version (KJV/NKJV), and the Living Bible or Message Bible, which are more of an interpretation or loose translation. These different renderings of the text should allow the reader to make comparisons and detect minor or major differences in the translated text. Keep in mind that all translations are at least partially subjective because they make an axis through the experience of those doing the translating. There is no pure objective translation because human beings are impure subjective entities with biases, emotions, preferences, distinct personalities, and prejudices. All of these human psychological traits tend to make their way into the original translation of the Greek or Hebrew text as well as into the modern translated English Bible.

After reading the text in five or six versions (or as many versions as is deemed reasonable), the preacher should then try to get a good *sense* of the text. This is what I call a first sense of the text, a "naïve sense,"[10] and an even more naïve understanding of the text. Here we experience the sheer or pure "pleasure of the text."[11] This is the prelude to a full understanding of the text that manifests itself aesthetically as a mental and physical feeling for the text or a textual aestheticism. This is a spiritual and emotional connection with the text—a chasing after its meaning. This process can be construed as a type of textual ecstasy that will lead to the development of a powerful textual sermon. But, as I said, the preacher has to lose herself or himself in the reading and re-reading of the text and allow the text to explode into every fiber of the human mind and body. This explosion provides what can only be described as a type of spiritual pleasure, a losing oneself in the gripping and groping arms of the text—a "textacy," according to Roland Barthes.[12]

This groping power of the text is akin to how the Old Testament prophet Isaiah speaks and how poet and writer Richard Wright, the Harlem Renaissance phenom, speaks in his epoch-making autobiography *Black Boy*. But more importantly, the spirit of this word, *grope,* as I use it, is captured by the author of the book of Job, who writes, "They grope in the dark without light; he makes them stagger like a drunkard." (12:25 NRSV), and "They meet with darkness in the daytime, and grope at noonday as in the night" (5:14 NRSV). Thus the groping arms of the scripture text should capture and captivate the preacher and raise the sermon to new heights, like the towering strength of the white oak and cedar trees or the sleek, captivating beauty of the towering California redwood.

This groping is the first step in the multifaceted process of getting in front of the text. It is important to emphasize that after reading the text silently to oneself, now the text has to be read aloud, as a type of speaking

---

10. See Paul Ricoeur, *The Symbolism of Evil* (Boston: Beacon, 1967) and *Interpretation Theory* (Fort Worth: Texas Christian University Press, 1976), 19–22.

11. See Roland Barthes, *The Pleasure of the Text* (New York: Farrar, Straus and Giroux, 1975).

12. See Roland Barthes, "Theory of the Text," in *Untying the Text*, ed. Robert Young (New York: Routledge, 1990), 33.

or speech act. The oralizing of the text is another element in the prelude to understand the scripture text, which is a necessary precondition to explanation in the sermon. Understanding both precedes and follows explanation.[13] In other words, the preacher reads to understand from the very beginning what he or she cannot explain in speech or writing, in the pulpit, or in the public square. This means that the preacher cannot explain that which he or she does not understand. When you interpret yourself, as opposed to understanding yourself, you are always advancing the self in ways that show a lack of self-knowledge. To understand one's self is a journey toward knowing the self. This means that the struggle for self-understanding often escapes our explanation. Explaining looks backward and understanding looks forward. This is prophetic and transforming.

Jonah is a perfect example. Understanding a text is a hard nut to crack because misunderstanding tends to be much more normative than understanding. One could say misunderstanding is the first step in understanding. Understanding a scripture text requires hard work—praying, reading, and studying. "The text then becomes the very object of hermeneutics,"[14] especially since hermeneutics deals with interpretation of texts and overcoming the distance between the writer of the text and the reader of the text. And the preacher is a text too—a complicated text—and so is the congregation. Overcoming the distance between the scripture chosen by the preacher and what the preacher has to say about the text in the sermon is the hermeneutic challenge or the meaning of interpretation in preaching. This means that the preacher is compelled to deal seriously with the chosen text—not as a pretext, or something to "tag" your sermon to or "If I had to have a text, let's use this one." It must be a genuine commitment to deciphering meaning and forming new meaning in the newly created sermonic message that itself will become a new text to be interpreted and understood.

Unfortunately, there is a visible and palpable effort on the part of the preacher to dance, skip, and jump around the chosen text, to deal with anything and everything under the sun except the text that she or he

13. See Ricoeur, *Interpretation Theory*, 71–89.
14. Barthes, "Theory of the Text," 33.

has voluntarily chosen. This is confounding to me as I listen to sermon after sermon, year in and year out. There is no problem in choosing a text. The preacher can choose a text with confidence, comfort, and ease. What I find disturbing is the preacher's quick and unabashed willingness to pretend to have a commitment to the text by choosing it, but then to abandon the text five minutes into the sermon. This is textual abandonment.

By this, I mean that there is a powerful proclivity to push the text aside and put in its place a pious platitude, such as, "um"; a misplaced vector away from the substance of the text, "Ah you don't hear me"; or even a song to try to save the sermon from death by switching from the chosen text and reverting into the all-too-familiar territory of abandoning the text for a proven, almost predictable, and possibly predatory solicitation of a self-serving response. This is predatory preaching designed to satiate the self. Response to the sermon should be natural and, if possible, unsolicited. But if it must be solicited, let it be solicited for something said that is meaningful, textual, and transformative. Preaching and reading are one. No reading, no preaching.

The scripture text itself should mediate against the tendency of the preacher to ignore the presence of the text by meandering into something other than the development of the text. This is so easy to do. To abandon the scripture text today has become an everyday occurrence. Almost every time the preacher says, "Turn to this text or that text" in an effort to explain the chosen text without developing and wrestling with the chosen pericope, he or she is engaging in the abandonment of the chosen text in favor of another text that itself begs to be interpreted. This meandering often contributes little or nothing to the understanding of the chosen text for this particular sermon.

What I mean here is that sticking with interpreting the chosen text is a serious and hard job that cannot be obfuscated through deliberate, disheartening distractions or through histrionic acrobatics and rhetorical flair like rhyming, alliteration, and allegory that does little to add to textual understanding, explanation, and sermonic transformation. The text is a weapon and a hedge against rhetoric's tendency to play tricks on the hearer.[15] and any other tricks of the preaching trade, including the wiles of the devil. Such tricks serve no purpose for the preacher to try to trick the congregation into believing that he or she is getting something that they are not getting. I think people are as adept in recognizing and identifying the tricks of the preacher as the preacher is in doing them.

More importantly, the development of the sermon demands a type of seriousness and commitment to excellence that all preachers must strive to achieve. There are no shortcuts and no easy ways to get around the long struggles and hard work of preaching powerful, meaningful, and transformative sermons. When you take shortcuts, you may be shortchanging yourself. Textual abandonment makes the preacher a liar—as much of a liar as Rev. Ambrose says he is in the Ernest Gaines novel, *A Lesson Before Dying*. In the novel, Rev. Ambrose says, "I lie, I lie, and I lie." His lying and our lying are not the same, but they are closely related.

The reading of the text should be done slowly, deliberately, and carefully. Every word has significance, which is the text in action and the text at work in service to the development of a powerful, transforming, even prophetic sermon. This means that the preacher is compelled to put herself or himself into the text, experiencing a total body and mind encounter with the text itself, resulting in a losing of oneself into the joy of the text, that is, the experience of the disruptive, regenerative nature of the scripture text.

Black preaching, for example, is not simply an emotional histrionic enterprise, as some scholars and preachers apparently tend to think. It is clearly emotional, but it is so much more than just emotion. It is knowledge. It is love. Preaching should not be characterized only by certain stylistics or preaching antics devoid of doxological and theological content and depth. Preaching cannot be reduced to a certain or particular method, whether that method claims to be expository, dialectical, correlation, narrative, or application. Method is very important, but the sermon is not limited to any of these particular methods. Method alone does not a sermon make!

---

15. See for example: Barthes, "Theory of the Text."

Black preaching is not only a spiritual endeavor, a spirit-filled action grounded in the aesthetics of rhythm and cadence, tonality and "tuning," and the fervor of beautiful words, but Black preaching also is first and foremost a function of the brain in all of its fluidity and dimensionality. It is a function of the "plasticity" of the brain, to use the language of philosopher Catherine Malabou.[16] By this, I mean that preaching in the spirit of a preacher like Nat Turner, John Jasper, "Black Harry" Hoosier, and Fannie Lou Hamer should be adaptable and creative—reading and speaking the text over and over *ad infinitum* and, if necessary, *ad nauseam*, until it saturates your pores and embeds itself into every fiber of your being. John Jasper's sermon "De Sun Do Move" and "De Earth Am Square," though patently illogical and scientifically unsound, is nevertheless a symbol of the creative and poetic power of the Black preacher. The poetic nature of the title alone is very captivating and compelling: "De Sun Do Move." Not only must there be a reading and re-reading of the scriptural text, but there has to be a listening to and hearing and rehearing of the text as well. Also, an un-reading of the text is necessary as I shall discuss in detail in chapter five.

Reading the text aloud provides an intentional listening to the voice or voices of the text, such that its voice is not drowned out or quelled by the loudness of more popular and dominating voices—those of writers of commentaries, popular pulpiteers, and other public-square theologians and preachers. This means that the preacher should always develop, write, and deliver his or her own sermons in his or her own language and voice, not unnecessarily imitating more popular, well-known, telegenic, and televised preachers. This is difficult because it is hard to find your own authentic voice when there are so many voices that you can imitate, that you imagine sound better than yours. And, in fact may sound better, but it is an uncertain sound because it is not your own.

It is better to struggle with the scripture text for yourself than to copy, borrow, steal, or deliver a sermon written and preached by someone else as if it were your own. That practice is, in fact, unethical, and for that

---

16. See Catherine Malabou, *What Should We Do with Our Brain* (New York: Fordham University Press, 2008); *Plasticity at the Dusk of Writing: Dialectic, Destruction, Deconstruction*, trans. Carolyn Shread (New York: Columbia University Press, 2009).

the preacher does need healing. Even in this internet, Snapchat, YouTube age, this is still plagiarism. It is thievery and a violation of your call to preach! More than that, it is inauthentic and, ultimately, it is ungodly and unholy. I repeat myself and redundantly say again: it is a gross violation of your call and commitment to preach. It is the opposite of what you want to be and how you want to represent the goodness and grace of God. It is indeed a cheap understanding of the costly grace of God, as the German theologian and pastor Dietrich Bonhoeffer said.[17] Scripture mandates "Make an effort to present yourself to God as a tried-and-true worker, who doesn't need to be ashamed but is one who interprets the message of truth correctly" (2 Tim 2:15). No matter your strengths or limitations, it is better for you, the community, and your church that you struggle with and write your own sermons. Just as the slaves preferred to hear their own preachers even in their broken English and unsystematic theology, Black church folk still prefer to hear their pastor preach his or her own sermons, than to have you steal them from somebody else and impose them upon yourself and your congregational context and the larger community.

The sermon must be your own sermon and the result of your own interpretation struggles with the text—your struggle with the self, community, and church; the result of your fasting, praying, studying, and reading; your battle with nuances, inconsistencies of thought, gaps in the text, and the intertextual nature of most scripture texts. Only then can your sermon show how the chosen text is influenced and impacted by other texts, including yourself and your congregation as text. If you do not believe my serious perspective on this issue, my thinking is that you will get caught in the entanglement of the internet for sermon preparation.

As a textual preacher, you are inevitably and inescapably involved in the art and science of hermeneutics or interpretation. You are interpreting the text from start to finish every time you write a sermon and every time you stand up to preach. You have to work hard and do your best with every sermon because all interpretations are not equal, which means that all sermons are not equal. Some are not ready for public disclosure. Some

---

17. Cf. Dietrich Bonhoeffer, *The Cost of Discipleship* (New York: Macmilllian, 1959).

should never see the light of day. And some are not close to the mark. This text that looks, sounds, feels, smells, and presents itself as foreign has to be made your own before it can be developed into a viable, powerful, transformative sermon.

Ricoeur says that to:

> make one's own what was previously 'foreign' remains the ultimate aim of all hermeneutics. Interpretation in its last stage wants to equalize, to render contemporaneous, to assimilate in the sense of making similar. This goal is achieved insofar as interpretation actualizes the meaning of the text for the present reader.[18]

Make the sermon your own! And I claim that it will make you its own! This means that plagiarism and stealing somebody else's sermon is off limits. The plagiarized (stolen) sermon is NOT your own! To make the sermon your own is a difficult and honest effort—the result of your own hard work. If you make the sermon your own, I guarantee that the sermon will claim you and mark you as a preacher from that day forward. A well-crafted sermon skillfully delivered helps to make you a preacher. It is not your licensure. It is not your ordination. It is not your well-earned degrees or continuing education certificates. It is not your legacy or your being from a family of preachers. No, it is the sermon itself! The sermon has the power to transform the poor, paltry preacher into a powerful, prophetic preacher, like the prophets Jeremiah, Isaiah, and Amos. Like our own scholars and prophets Samuel DeWitt Proctor, Miles Jerome Jones, Gardner C. Taylor, Ella Mitchell, Harry S. Wright, and Patricia Gould-Champ. Like young new voices, such as Charlotte McSwine-Harris, Lisa Lawrence Wilson, and Dwayne Whitehead. Like the millennial voices of Amanda Harper, Joshua Mitchell, Tony Baugh, and Eric Gill. It is the sermon that has the power to make the preacher over and over, again and again. I cannot say it enough: the well-crafted sermon has the power to transform the preacher into a brand new being—a new creation, as the Apostle Paul says (cf. 2 Cor 5:17).

18. Ricoeur, *Interpretation Theory*, 91.

Reading and Studying as Acts of Holiness— Requisites for Getting in Front of the Text

The idea of the holy is one thing. The practice of holiness is another. It takes a high degree of spiritual and psychological discipline to understand and practice reading and studying as serious spiritual acts of holiness as a prelude to getting in front of the text. This means that if you claim to be or want to become a preacher, then you should be reading and studying the text and something related or unrelated to the text.

Nobody in the church or in your household is going to make you do this. Not the bishop. Not the elders. Not the amour bearers. Not the deacons. Not the trustees. Not the church mothers or anybody else. You might even be discouraged from reading and studying by some of these church folk who believe that the sermon should be "divined and guessed at," as if this is the real meaning of the Holy Spirit. I cannot count the times that my church officers and church members have told me that I did not need to go to school anymore or that too much study is counter-productive. On the whole, this is a bald-faced fallacy, and the preacher needs to counter this by setting aside some time every day to read and study. This includes reading and studying literature and novels, like *Go Tell It On the Mountain* by James Baldwin, *A Lesson Before Dying* by Ernest Gaines, *All Aunt Hagar's Children* by Edward P. Jones, *Beloved* and *The Bluest Eye* by Toni Morrison, *Passing* by Nella Larsen, *The Stranger* and *The Fall* by Albert Camus, *Gilead* by Marilynne Robinson, and *I Know Why the Caged Bird Sings* by Maya Angelou. Read short stories, biographies, history, poetry, literature, theology, published sermons and papers, and for God's sake, read the Bible. This has to become a doxological practice, a *habitus*, a routine act, a ritual observed as faithfully as the Lenten fast or the first Sunday communion in Black Baptist, African Methodist Episcopal (Zion), and Pentecostal churches. People assume that inspiration rules out the need to study and prepare, but there is a need for both.

The more the preacher reads and studies, the more powerful and transformative the sermon becomes and the greater the possibility of getting in front of the text. Ricoeur states in no uncertain terms,

35

The sense of a text is not behind the text, but in front of it. It is not something hidden, but something disclosed. What has to be understood is not the initial situation of discourse, but what points toward a possible world, thanks to the non-ostensive reference of the text. Understanding has less than ever to do with the author and his situation. It seeks to grasp the world-propositions opened up by the reference of the text. To understand a text is to follow its movement from sense to reference: from what it says, to what it talks about.[19]

Wow! Getting in front of the text is exactly where the text wants—even begs—the preacher to be. And more importantly, the text has less to do with the author than it does with you—the preacher and the hearer. The author of the text is dead and cannot, in any possible way, explain what has been written. This means that the preacher really only has the text itself and the sense of the text that will help him or her understand the text. This sense of the text is not something to be found in the archives of history or among the stacks of ancient and modern commentaries. No!

It is not hidden among the ideas of the great church fathers like Augustine, Ambrose, and Tertullian, or the theologians like Karl Barth, Paul Tillich, and James Cone, or philosophers like Enrique Dussel. No! It is not buried deep in the language and the syntax of the ancient Greeks and the Epicureans. No!

You dig and dig in those hidden places to no avail. Meaning is not a treasure hidden behind the curtain of the theological and biblical wizard, or at the bottom of the Red or Dead Sea, or among the ancient ruins of Egypt and Mesopotamia. Meaning is not hidden behind anything except a lack of study and imagination. It's there to be disclosed. And you and I, the modern-day preachers, have to disclose what is there, and by implication, what is not there by getting in front of the text.

The meaning of the text, then, discloses itself in the newness of the unfolding future,[20] a future that is now revealing and disclosing itself in the study and at the point of utterance by the preacher. The most important element in asserting (like Ricoeur) that "the meaning of the text

19. Ricoeur, *Interpretation Theory*, 87–88.
20. Cf. Martin Heidegger's notion of the "future bearing down on us."

is in front of it" is to understand that the "disclosure" is a reference to a possible world. The text reveals and discloses a new world. A free world. A world without violence and racial hatred. A world without children dying of hunger and disease. A world where bombs and guns are no longer pandemic purveyors of death and destruction. A world where we study war no more, and our swords are beaten into plowshares.

The text speaks of a possible world. A "not yet" world. To get in front of the text is to believe the simple, yet transformative dictum that "all things are possible." This possible world reflects the spirit and imagination of the visionary, prophetic, and proleptic nature of the text bearing down upon us like beams of heaven, like hope unborn, like shouts of joy. The text points to something other than what is past and even already present. The text points to the edge of something new—something ahead of itself, not something hidden behind it. It's something unfolding, something that "ain't" never even been dreamed of or seen before.

But now, because of this text, I can understand that there is a river flowing with life-giving water. Because of the disclosure of this text, I can declare to the people of God that there is a bright side somewhere; there is a fountain filled with blood. There is a word from the Lord. There is a balm in Gilead. There is a world, a possible world, where there is no more racism. There is a world, a possible world, where there is no more injustice, no more hatred, no more sleepless nights. There is a world, a possible world, where there is no more killing of Black male and female youth, no more aimless and hopeless men and women, no more drunken torpor, no more wars and rumors of wars. The text points toward these possibilities because that world, that possible world, is the referential world of the text with the power to transform and create a brand new world. This is where hope unborn comes to life. This is where dry bones can live again. This is where the preacher's textual imagination creates a new possibility of freedom.

Understanding the text and explaining the text, preaching the text and getting in front of the text, is the meaning of preaching forward and preaching transformation. To be transformed is to become something more than what you are—something and someone totally and completely different from your current state of being. To be transformed is exactly what Franz Kafka depicted in the *Metamorphosis* when Gregor Samsa went to sleep as one thing and woke up completely transformed into something else. Something other than what he was. A new being. While this is not a happy example of becoming a "new being," it is a gross example of cataclysmic change. Hans Gadamer calls it transformation. And it is akin to what the Apostle Paul meant when he wrote, "Don't be conformed to the patterns of this world, but be transformed by the renewing of your minds so that you can figure out what God's will is—what is good and pleasing and mature" (Rom 12:2). That's akin to the experience of encountering Jesus Christ where you are right now. You could be transformed from a swigging and swilling, backstabbing and brawling brother or sister into somebody sitting clothed and in your right mind, like the man who lived among the tombs until he encountered the transforming power of Jesus Christ in the Gospels of Mark and Luke. (cf. Mark 5:1-20 and Luke 8:26-39).

Let us take a particular scripture text in an effort to demonstrate how to get in front of the text. It is the familiar story in the Gospel of Luke.

> One day he got into a boat with his disciples, and he said to them, "Let us go across to the other side of the lake." So they put out, and while they were sailing he fell asleep. A windstorm swept down on the lake, and the boat was filling with water, and they were in danger. They went to him and woke him up, shouting, "Master, Master, we are perishing!" And he woke up and rebuked the wind and the raging waves; they ceased, and there was a calm. He said to them, "Where is your faith?" They were afraid and amazed, and said to one another, "Who then is this, that he commands even the winds and the water, and they obey him?" (8:22-25 NRSV)

In reading, re-reading, and un-reading this scripture, I have developed a new understanding and interpretation of Jesus calming the storm. This text is not about any of the surface issues that seem to be going on in this scene. The chaos and the calm are all relevant but not essential. It is certainly not about the storm. That is the occasion for the story, but the storm is *not* the story. That is ancillary. It is not about the sea, the wind, the waves, or the firmament. That is secondary. It is not about faith or fear. It is not about the size of the boat or even the power of the storm or calming of the raging sea. That is tertiary. The sermon has no time to waste on those textual issues that are ancillary, secondary, and tertiary. All of that is certainly behind the text, and it is very good to know, but we have to get in front of this text by understanding what else—what is crucial, what is essential, what is transformative—that this text reveals to us. It is not about all the rest, which indeed may be important, but it just is not decisive. It is clutter. Do not clutter your sermon with unnecessary stuff and fluff.

This text, in my view, is really about the issue of identity. It is pointing to an understanding of the identity and meaning of Jesus as the Christ. So, the sermon must focus on this very critical and decisive understanding of the text, which moves us beyond chaos and calmness to a new level of meaning. The identity question is still hanging out there: "Who then is this?" This is the epistemic moment, a new and disclosive opportunity to reconcile the dialectic between knowing and event, between speech and act. Getting in front of the text means that the preacher has to understand that Jesus has already commanded that the chaos of the violent and unruly storm cease. That is done! That is over! Jesus has spoken, and the wind and the sea have already been made mute. This chaos, this noise, these rumblings have been silenced and sequestered by the call for peace and stillness. Jesus's speech has obviated and silenced the outspoken, howling, and boisterous sounds of the wind and the waves. Jesus is the voice, the speech, the Logos, and the power of God.

This event, like all events, would pass away like the withering of grass or the fading of flowers, but how this event is understood and explained— and what this event means—becomes the foundation and the starting-point the embryonic formation for preaching the gospel. The disciples' question to each other, though grounded in a thick disconnect and distance between them and Jesus, is a question that must be answered. We have to get in front of this text and try to understand what world it is unveiling to us right now. I can see this possible world. Can you see it? Oh, my beloved brothers and sisters, the disclosive nature of this text is bubbling to the surface of my imagination, causing me to reflect on what is being disclosed, being revealed, being referenced by this text.

Your family is well. Your children are all healthy and safe. You have been in the hospital and now you are back home. You have been in the chaos, in the storm, and through the storm. Chaos. You have had surgery, and now you are on the mend. You can walk again; you have the use of your limbs and you are still in your right mind. Your speech is no longer slurred. The doctor has given you a clean bill of health. You have a job, and your bills are now being paid by the sweat of your own hand. The storm is over, and like the disciples of Jesus in this Lukan text, you are still asking, "Who is this that commands the winds and the waves and they obey?"

Allow me to interrupt myself and confess that I have a certain vagueness, a certain denseness, about some questions of understanding and misunderstanding that linger in my weak, struggling, frail, and faltering mind. I may not fully understand Friedrich Schleiermacher's *Hermeneutics: The Handwritten Manuscripts*; I may not understand Immanuel Kant's rational religion; I may not understand Franz Kafka's *Metamorphosis*; I may not understand Hans Gadamer's *Truth and Method*, or Martin Heidegger's *Being and Time*. I may not understand abstract analytical philosophy as well as I should, and there is a whole lot of other stuff and people that I do not understand, but on the question of "Who then is this?" I do have something to say in the language and spirit of the Black preacher and my practice of getting in front of the text.

If you do not know who woke you up this morning and who put food on your table, and if you do not know who worked a miracle in your life—who took the taste of alcohol from your lips, who stopped you from drinking and driving and saved you from yourself—if you do not know today who picked you up and turned your life around, then how can I try to get you in front of the text, to step in front in order to assure you that it was not Sigmund Freud or Karl Jung or Dr. Phil or Dr. Oz? It was not your id or ego or superego. It was not your palm reader or soothsayer. It was not your own frail and weak wisdom. It was not your family, and it was not your economic status. Who then is this who has created a sense of wholeness in your mind and in your body? Who then is this who has calmed your fears and brought serenity and peace to your life? Who then is this?

Can I try to get in front of the text? Can I answer for the doubting disciples who are focusing on the storm? Can I answer for the ones who have been to the "mourner's bench," those who have been baptized, those "who have come a mighty long way," those who are afraid to speak, those who are still unable to recognize clearly or even vaguely the power and presence of God? *Who then is this?* Can I get out front, in front of the text, and help us to understand that the meaning of the text is not behind it, but in front of it, addressing me, addressing you? Who then is this? His name is Jesus. Who then is this? He is Messiah. Who then is this? He is King of Kings and Lord of Lords. Who then is this? He is Isaiah's comforter and Mark's messianic secret. Who then is this? He is John's revelation and Paul's message of grace. Who then is this?[21]

JONAH II: "Pursued by Greatness"

> But the LORD *hurled a great wind upon the sea,*
> *and such a mighty storm came upon the sea,*
> *that the ship threatened to break up [...]*
> *So [the sailors] picked up Jonah and threw him into the sea [...]*
> *But the LORD provided a large fish to swallow up Jonah;*
> *and Jonah was in the belly of the fish three days and three nights.*
>
> —Jonah 1:4, 15, 17

Almost all of us want to be great. We have that latent desire to be a star. We aspire to be somebody like LeBron James, Peyton Manning, Russell Westbrook, and Russell Wilson. Oh, how can I forget Michael Jordan? Some generations, in their youth, wanted to be Michael Jordan so badly that we went out and bought expensive tennis shoes with Jordan's image on them in some illogical belief that we could then jump in the air and shoot the basketball like Jordan. Girls want to be great too, like Serena Williams, Angela Bassett, or Beyoncé. All of us are in pursuit of "greatness."

---

21. James Henry Harris, *The Word Made Plain: The Power and Promise of Preaching* (Minneapolis: Fortress, 2004), 140–46.

41

And, we think they are the same—greatness as celebrity and greatness as seeking God's purpose in our life. They might come together, but often they can be in tension with each other. We want to be a great musician like J. Cole or Jay Z, or Rhianna or a great actor like Denzel Washington, Halle Berry, Morgan Freeman, or Viola Davis. Greatness, meaning the desire to be perceived and thought of as something special, seems to be what drives us. And do not get me wrong, that is good. Our young Black boys and girls need to focus on achievement, excelling in school, doing their homework, studying, practicing, praying and preparing themselves in every way possible. We have enough negativity and evil. We need to get out of their path and let them reach for greatness in whatever we are trying to do.

But it's one thing to pursue aesthetic greatness by chasing after the mighty dollar, driven by greed and vulgar capitalism, and becoming a type of slave to more and more, bigger and bigger things. Not only can you not serve God and money, you cannot serve money either! Now, I know that some of you are trying to make ends meet, trying to get enough money to go back to school for one more semester. I know that some have become addicted at a very young age to technology—to cell phones, iPads, and the like. Some of these gadgets are potentially good because they advance the use of technology in a way that delivers convenience. But let us not become so dependent, so addicted to technology or another substance that we forget how to use our brains to add, multiply, subtract, and divide. To count money. To read a book. To think. The movie *Lucy*, while laden with violence, drugs, and corruption, is mainly about the fact that we do not know what to do with our brains. We are so quick to limit our own capacity. We are using less than 10 percent of our brains capacity. *Lucy* and French philosopher Catherine Malabou are trying to press us forward to new frontiers. Stretch your mind. Use your imagination. Dream. Think new thoughts. Conquer new worlds by broadening your horizons.

In our text, Jonah is trying his best to flee from the greatness of the Lord. This young prophet is trying to get away from the Lord's presence, like so many in the church today. Jonah is, in fact, pursuing something else. He is in pursuit of anonymity. He is pursuing his own agenda. He is following his own ambitions. He is uninterested in what the Lord asked him to do. He is pretty pig headed, bull-headed, strong headed, strong willed, foolish, angry and, displaying an ugly attitude – am I on your street yet? Ok, what about, he is just plain disobedient, running away from God because he thought that he knew more than God.

God did not go to your college, and God did not study economics, science, psychology, English, and computer engineering. We say, "God cannot tell me what to do, what to say, and to whom to say it. I am my own person. I got my driver's license. I got my diploma. I got a job. I got a car and the loan papers show that I am grown now, so I am going to Joppa, to New York. I am going to Norfolk, New Orleans, Miami, to where I want to go. I ain't going to Nineveh to get them people upset with me, because then the Lord turns around and forgives them of 'they' sins. And I will be left out in the cold, looking like a fool." That is how Jonah thought.

Jonah, my beloved brothers and sisters, is being pursued by the greatness of God. The greatness of God's mercy and the greatness of God's loving-kindness are in hot pursuit of Jonah. It may not seem like it on first glimpse because so much chaos surrounds all of this.

When you are pursued by the greatness of God, you will have to go through some heavy times and may put others through some heavy stuff because of your actions and your decisions. Your bad decisions don't keep God from pursuing you out of love and mercy. The text says, "But the LORD hurled a great wind upon the sea, and such a mighty storm came upon the sea that the ship threatened to break up. Then the mariners were afraid, and each cried to his god. They threw the cargo that was in the ship into the sea, to lighten it for them" (1:4-5 NRSV). When nothing seemed to help, they decided that Jonah was the problem; so, after much wrangling and a lot of prayer, they "picked Jonah up and threw him into the sea; and the sea ceased from its raging" (v. 15).

When you are pursued by greatness, there is nowhere to hide, nowhere to run, nowhere to escape. There is no ship large enough to keep you away from God. No sailors, no cargo can shield you from God. And this is the loving-kindness of God. This is the mercy and grace of God.

This text teaches us also that in being pursued by greatness, the Lord will provide. God was providing for Jonah the whole time he was being disobedient. The whole time he was running away from the Lord, the Lord was making it possible for him to be saved. God is inescapable. "The LORD is great and so worthy of praise! God's greatness can't be grasped" (Ps 145:3).

When we are pursued by greatness, and this greatness is the Lord, the Lord will provide. You may not know how you are going to make it. You lost your job. You cannot pay your rent. You do not know how you are going back to college. You owe money from last semester and the term before that. You got a bad doctor's report. People have treated you like the sailors treated Jonah. Your family may have turned their backs on you. Your cousins, your children, your spouse, your friends may have thrown you into the sea, into the abyss. I tell you that you may have been treated like Jonah, thrown overboard by the church, the school, the family, the Boys and Girls Club.

Sometimes, if you are the problem, you have got to be dealt with—and dealt with harshly. Thrown overboard for the sake of the safety of others on the ship. For the sake of the church. For the sake of the community, for the sake of others. For the sake of yourself. After Jonah was thrown overboard into the angry sea, the very next verse of our text says, "But the LORD provided a large fish to swallow up Jonah; and Jonah was in the belly of the fish three days and three nights" (v. 17, emphasis added). Wow! What a story. What a miracle.

Chapter Two
RE-READING

The Preacher as Poet and Writer of the Word

JONAH III: "Second Chances"

> *The word of the LORD came to Jonah a second time,*
> *saying "Get up, go to Nineveh,*
> *that great city, and proclaim to it the message that I tell you."*
> *So Jonah set out and went to Nineveh, according to the word of the LORD.*

—Jonah 3:1-10 (NRSV)

Many of us today have wasted and squandered time, money, and opportunities. We have faltered and failed in so many ways to do what God has called us to do. And yet we have so little compassion when it comes to the faults of others. It seems that we are quick to condemn and even eager to accuse, to point a finger and judge someone else for their human weaknesses, their failures, their slips of conscience, and their acquiescence to the luring pleasure power of the flesh. We have a condemning air about us, an arrogant spirit of superiority that suggests that we have never done anything wrong, that we have never lied, never fornicated or committed adultery, never deceived or tricked or schemed, never been homeless or poor or hungry. We act as if we are perfect and everybody else is in need of salvation—everybody except us. Jonah teaches us that we are not perfect, that life includes failure, and if we are going to be sane, we have to learn

45

to cope with the ups and downs of life. Jonah is the epitome of human arrogance and frailty.

Jonah disobeyed God; he ignored the call of God. He went in the wrong direction, was thrown overboard, and was swallowed up by a big fish. Jonah has been to hell and back. He has been in the deep, dark, dank dungeons of Sheol—but God was still there. You can run from God, but you cannot get away from God. And while folk in the pews and in the choir stands may be slow to forgive and quick to judge their fellow brothers and sisters, God is a God of second chances. God does not write us off even if we go in the wrong direction, go down the wrong path, get on the wrong boat, and cause chaos and stormy weather for others.

Yes, Jonah was disobedient, and yes, Jonah was hard-headed. He was obstinate and ugly in his behavior and attitude. Yes, Jonah was determined to disobey God and disregard the word of the Lord. But then the sweetest, most gracious words of scripture are found in this text, the words that describe the essential nature of God: a God who gives second chances. So I implore you, do not write people off, do not be unforgiving, do not be mad and unkind, and do not be rigid and inflexible in your relationship with others. Give folk a second chance! God is a God of second chances. Let us look at the text more closely to learn a few lessons from it.

We glean from the text that the message of the Lord is the same the second time around. Second chances do not mean that the message has changed. Jonah 3:1-2 says, "The word of the LORD came to Jonah a *second time* saying, 'Get up, go to Nineveh that great city...'" It may take a re-reading to understand that the assignment has not changed. The mission and the mandate are still the same: go to Nineveh. The destination is the same; the place that we ran from the first time is still the place where God wants us to go. Just because Jonah took an excursion on the Mediterranean Sea and caused a lot of havoc does not mean that his orders from God have changed. Just because he had gone AWOL did not mean that God had changed his orders – and although he had said "no" the first time, when God came to him the second time God said the same thing: "Go to Nineveh! Do what I ask you to do, go to the jails and prisons, go to the schools and street corners, go to those who are hopeless, go to

Nineveh, that great city—go to the place where the need is great, where the power brokers reside, go to Nineveh. Go where I send you."

Second chances give us an opportunity to do what we did not do the first time. Not only is Jonah to go to Nineveh, but he is told to do the same thing God told him the first time: "Preach! Proclaim the message that I tell you!" God wanted Jonah to preach—not to philosophize or rationalize, but to preach! Not to sing or to testify, but to preach! Not counsel or give advice, but to preach! Not to entertain or indulge folk in their carnality, in their baneful and base behaviors, but to preach. Not to come in timidity and in fear, but to preach, boldly proclaiming the word of God. Jonah was not sent to do anything but preach.

Not only was Jonah to preach, but the Lord said he will tell him the message. When God sends you, God will prepare you—not necessarily by divine revelation but by serious preparation, by searching and studying, by reason and experience, and by re-reading. All of this leads to re-reading which leads to a better sermon. It might be that Jonah is ready now to declare God's message of salvation. Jonah is ready now the second time around to preach the message of forgiveness. After being in the belly of the big fish, Jonah has a new consciousness, a new understanding of the love and grace of God. Jonah now understands God's omnipotence, that God is the God of land and sea. He can now proclaim to the people in the great city of Nineveh that God is love, that God hears prayers, that God can rescue you from the clutches of death and give you a second chance.

And this time you can preach what the Lord tells you to preach, not what you want to say. Not what folk want to hear, not what tickles the fancy and satisfies the power brokers in the church and community, but you too can preach what God tells you. Proclaim what you have endured, what you have witnessed, what you have experienced, what you know in your soul. Proclaim not what somebody else is saying, preach not what you learned about German philosophy or Reformed theology—not Immanuel Kant, G. W. F. Hegel, Martin Luther, or even John Calvin, for that matter. Preach what God tells you. Beloved, I do not have a message of my own. I do not have anything to say to the church on my own. I'm too weak, too selfish; I am too rational; I am too afraid; I am too rebellious; I am too

47

ignorant; I am too much of a failure like Jonah to have a message of my own. I must proclaim the message that God tells me to preach!

Second chances enable us to turn our "no" into a "yes." In Jonah 1, when the word of the Lord came to Jonah and called him to Nineveh, Jonah said "no" and fled from the presence of the Lord. But now, after all he has been through, now Jonah has a second chance and he says, "Yes, Lord. I will go where you tell me to go!" Yes, Lord, I will say what you tell me to say because when I did what I wanted to do, I failed. When I did what I wanted to do, I almost died. When I did what I wanted to do, I almost destroyed others. When I did what I wanted to do, I lost my way. When I did what I wanted to do, I was sinking deep in sin, far from the peaceful shore. Now, Lord, I have a second chance, and I am going to use it to preach, to proclaim what you tell me to say.

God is a God of second chances. Folk have made foolish mistakes, but God used them again, gave them a second chance. Look at Abraham. He was willing to pass off his own wife as his sister. And when Abraham and Sarah had given up on having a son, God came to Abraham a second time. Look at, David, that great prophet. His unthinkable sin began with Bathsheba and ended with Uriah. Yet, God used Bathsheba to carry on the bloodline of the Messiah. And, David in some strange way is the "Jesus" of the Hebrew Bible.

Let us not forget, Simon Peter, who, in a moment of cowardly human weakness, said, "I don't know him!" (cf. Luke 22:57). Jesus had said, "I tell you, Peter, the rooster won't crow today before you have denied three times that you know me" (v. 34). Yet, on the day of Pentecost, God came to Peter a second time and Peter preached what he Lord told him to. Three thousand folk were converted (cf. Acts 2:41). Come here, Paul, ranting and raving against the church, standing in the crowd while Stephen was being stoned to death (cf. Acts 7:54-60). Yet on the road to Damascus, God came to him a second time (cf. Acts 9).

If God could use folk like that, folk like Jonah and Abraham, folk like Jacob and David, folk like Peter and Paul, I know he can use us. God is a second-chance God![1]

---

1. James Henry Harris, *The Word Made Plain: The Power and Promise of Preaching* (Minneapolis: Fortress, 2004), 140–46.

Getting in Front of the Text

Comfort, comfort my people!

—Isaiah 40:1

And how shall they preach, except they be sent? As it is written,
How beautiful are the feet of them that preach the gospel of peace,
and bring glad tidings of good things!

—Romans 10:15 (KJV)

The poet speaks volumes in a few choice and well-crafted words; indeed, so does any good writer. And the preacher, who is potentially both a poet and a writer, would do well to learn how to be a less wordy speaker and writer. Preachers must speak and write with precision and carefully chosen words, phrases, and sentences. Words and sentences are crafted by inspiration from the muse—the daughters of Zeus or from the God of Harriet Tubman and Sojourner Truth, the God of David and Solomon, of Matthew, Mark, and Luke. The poem is a tool to *socialize* the symbols of religious devotion and commitment; to *reveal* the symbols of good, evil, and corruption; and to *call forth* the transformation of an unjust and ungodly society. Again, I think of writers like James Baldwin and Langston Hughes, essayists and poets who spoke of the struggles and evils that saturate the heart, spirit, and mind of America. I think of W. E. B. Du Bois and how poetic and spiritual are the lines that open each chapter of *The Souls of Black Folk*. These socially conscious, cutting-edge poets and writers have been joined by others like Nikki Giovanni, Rita Dove, and Maya Angelou.

As for myself and the budding poet in me, I love how the darkness of night gives way to the bright morning star and the early light of the sun that challenges the moonlight just before daybreak. Just like the "potent coming of spring penetrates all nature with joy,"[2] the summer heat gives way to the cool breeze of the autumn air, fresh as the morning. It is something that I love, and yet, it is more lovely and beautiful than Shakespeare's summer's day. Every morning when I rise, I wonder if heaven could be so sweet, so calm, and so potent as the air that breezes through the trees touching ever

---

2. Friedrich Nietzsche, *The Birth of Tragedy* (Garden City, NY: Doubleday, 1956), 36.

so lightly, blowing the leaves upon the ground or the light of the sun that darts through the trees upon the leaves and dances and freckles the ground with its feckless power. As a preacher, I am inspired by poets and writers, even preachers as wide and varied as Nikki Giovanni, Missy Elliot, Patricia Smith, and Langston Hughes, and; by Martin Luther King Jr., Samuel DeWitt Proctor, and Toni Morrison; by Amiri Baraka and Maya Angelou, who have caused me to write my own poem inspired by Emily Dickinson's poem "A Thought Went Up My Mind Today."

Let me tell you a short, small story.
Yes, like me
It is both not too tall and not that small.
It is a personal story.
In the spirit of Emily Dickinson,
A thought also went up my mind today.
I was walking in the sun,
A gleaming brightness reflecting from the snow covered ground—

I thought of the work I had to do.
The papers and books to write.
I thought of the lectures I had to give
And the sermons that needed to be written and preached. I thought...
I thought a thought today.

Time goes so fast,
It outruns my days and my fleeting thoughts.
And even before time is past,
And after I pray and fast, the thought that climbed upon my mind today never lasts—
And if you are wondering about the story, If you are wondering about my story...
The plot, the beginning, the middle, and the ending.

Today, I have little more to say.
No real story.
No complete story.

Just a thought
That took its time to play
And not to stay in my mind
—At least not today.[3]

The Poetry of Humiliation and Exaltation

The humiliation of Black people is expressed throughout the poetry of Langston Hughes, but nowhere better than in his poem "Roland Hayes Beaten." Hughes writes: "Negros, Sweet and docil... / Beware the day they change their minds!"[4]

Allow me to explain or clarify further what I mean by getting in front of the text by explaining a little more of the relationship between scripture text, history, and culture as it relates to the meaning of revelation and hope for African Americans. In our history and culture, a history of chattel slavery characterized by the terror of the slave auction block and the Middle Passage, is a journey from the shores of West Africa to the plantations of the Americas. This history must never be forgotten, but it should not be romanticized either. This memory settles like sediment in our collective unconscious.

W. E. B. Du Bois describes Black religion in *The Souls of Black Folk* as having three distinct elements: the preacher, the music, and the frenzy in regards to the modern Black church experience. Each expresses the deep sufferings and sorrows of a people whose language had been extirpated from their memory. I have learned that I too only have one language, and that language is really not mine![5] As Black people, as descendants of former slaves, we have no memory of our original language because it was

---

3. Inspired by Emily Dickinson, "A Thought Went Up My Mind Today," in *The Complete Poems of Emily Dickinson* (Boston: Little, Brown, and Company, 1924).

4. This poem was published under the title "Warning" in Hughes's collection *The Panther & the Lash: Poems of Our Time,* 1st vintage classics ed. (New York: Random House, 1992), 100.

5. See Jacques Derrida, *Monolingualism of the Other* (Stanford: Stanford University Press, 1998). And yet, I mean something much more particular because of my assertion that Blacks are the hated Other, not so much because of language but because of race and the axis through American slavery. The slavery connection is still a residual correlative with hatred of Blacks in America.

violently erased from our consciousness, something that never happened to the Hebrews or the Greeks.

So, my feeling is that until I can recover my own language, I stubbornly and unconsciously, as well as consciously, refuse to learn another language that imitates the oppressor, whether it is the Greeks or the Romans, the Germans or the French. We have been humiliated and terrorized as a community and as individuals. In the sorrowful language of the Negro Spiritual, we have been "buked and we have been scorned." We have been talked about, ridiculed, and denied freedom and ontological status from Hegel's racist Eurocentrism (which often masquerades as logic and philosophy) to modern-day theorists, politicos, and talking heads saturating the airways with vitriol and hate.

I can feel and see the humiliation that Black people have endured, and it is expressed so eloquently by some of our preachers, poets, and writers. From Claude McKay's *Manchild in the Promised Land* to Richard Wright's *Black Boy*, and James Baldwin's *The Fire Next Time* to Nella Larsen's *Passing*, to Zora Neale Hurston's *Jonah's Gourd Vine* and *Their Eyes Were Watching God*, our humiliation and suffering have been catalogued. In films like *The Help*, *Django Unchained*, and *Lincoln*, the humiliation continues on many levels because neither Steven Spielberg nor Quentin Tarantino is Black, yet they are the ones chosen and funded to tell the Black story. This too is a form of humiliation by the exclusion of the Black storyteller, filmmaker, and writer. We are the humiliated Other. The "Other Other."

The preacher as poet is called to help mitigate against the pain and suffering endemic to Black life, Black religion, and culture. It must be done without comedy and without dance, but with truth and love because it is no laughing matter. The poem, like the sermon, is a sorrow song, a blues and spiritual song like "Were You There When They Crucified My Lord?"

The Apostle Paul introduces the need for a practical theology and wisdom in the community in his New Testament writings. He advises the Philippians to base their practical reasoning on that which they see in Jesus Christ: "Your attitude should be the same as that of Christ Jesus" (Phil 2:5 NIV). A Jesus who was bold enough to make himself of no reputation. A Jesus who was bold enough to empty himself of his "Godness" and become human (v. 6-11). A Jesus who took on the form of a servant, and being found in human form, humbled himself and became obedient, even unto death on a cross. This is what our Black slave foreparents understood.

For nearly three hundred years, folk were loaded and stacked on cargo ships and transported across the Atlantic from Central to West Africa (Congo-Angola, Nigeria, Dahomey, Togo, the Gold Coast, and Sierra Leone) to support the greed and evils of racism and capitalism of white Southern plantation owners. In spite of plantation owners' efforts to strip them of their religion, language, and culture, Black people were able to miraculously find in Christianity and other religions some semblance of spiritual and moral reasoning. They may not have seen it in most of Paul's theology, but they did see it in the New Testament's main character, Jesus Christ.

Blacks tend to identify with Jesus no matter how repulsive and oppressive language sounds and feels. There is an identification with Jesus as the humiliated human, Jesus as the hated Other, as one put to death on a cross or tree, as the song says, which is a symbol of lynching and suffering to most Blacks.[6] As Gayraud Wilmore attests in his now-classic text *Black Religion and Black Radicalism*, Black religion is indeed something more and something less than traditional American Christianity.[7]

Black folk know something about humiliation and suffering, something about trouble, and something about pain. Likewise, Jesus has been castigated and humiliated, according to the scripture. But it says in conclusion, "Therefore, God has highly exalted him and given him a name that is above every name" (v. 9). Herein lies the hope and the transformation.

The Poetic and the Aesthetic in the Life of Black Church Folk

My life is full of stories. Big stories. Little stories. Strong stories. Weak stories. Poetic and people stories. Let me tell you one.

---

6. For example, James H. Cone, *The Cross and the Lynching Tree* (Maryknoll, NY: Orbis Books, 2011).

7. Gayraud Wilmore, *Black Religion and Black Radicalism: An Interpretation of the Religious History of African Americans* (Maryknoll, NY: Orbis Books, 1998).

It was Sunday morning at a church in South Carolina not long ago, I remember it like it was yesterday. It was a packed service; men, women, and children sat close together. There were hats galore—reds, blues, greens, pinks, whites, burgundies, and yellows everywhere. People had come from far and near to witness the installation and celebration of a new pastor. The lady in the pew directly in front of me wore a red-and-white hat with a brim as wide as the wings of the seraphim, and the lady beside her was not any better. Together, their hats seemed to exceed the wing span of a Boeing 737, covering the length of the entire back pew. A lady sitting across the aisle was dressed in a blue-and-gold afghan, with pearls around her neck and matching earrings. But this was not what caught my attention and arrested my vision. It was the long-stemmed black gloves on her fingers, reaching all the way from the tip of her hands up to her elbows. I was struck by the sight of a black woman wearing long silk gloves to the Sunday service in this day and time. It was like yesterday was creeping back into today.

Yesterday's traditions and practices were seen all over the church. It was Communion Sunday, and the deacons were all dressed in dark suits of black, blue, and gray. They looked officious, old-school, and like the gray-haired nabob in Mark Twain's *Adventures of Huckleberry Finn*. They had on starched white shirts with white pocket handkerchiefs and seemed to be "professors of holy communion," tenured in the serving of the bread and the wine. The women, all dressed in linen dresses, were not allowed to touch the communion trays. There were no women deacons, just "deaconesses." Patriarchy still reigns supreme in many Black churches.

A week later, just after Easter Monday, another preacher was being consecrated into the high and holy office of bishop in the Pentecostal Church. I was honored that he had asked, a few months earlier, if his small church could have his big celebration in our church building because it was rather spacious and, more importantly, because his grandmother and his father had grown up as Baptists in the Second Baptist Church. I was happy to let them use the church building because it was so much a part of their personal history and the revelation of God in their lives and ours.

On that evening, I served as an usher—a doorkeeper—greeting people as they meandered through the doors of the church. Some spoke to me; others were too officious and highfalutin to part their lips or bow their heads as I held the door for them to enter the building. See, I was dressed extremely casual, sporting tennis shoes, jogging pants, and an exercise shirt. Some folk looked at me as if I were uninformed about the sacred formality of the event. Yet I wanted simply to serve as a hospitable host, though I did not have time to go home and change into more suitable attire.

As I held the door and welcomed folk dressed immaculately in white, purple, red, and black, their robes and gowns looking like they had been woven by the gifted hands of the women and men of Ghana, I too was feeling the pomp and circumstance of the event. The excitement was palpable and could be seen and felt a mile away. The service started out very traditional, with soft pipe organ music and a processional of preachers and potentates marching in step like the army of God. It was quite stylistic, aesthetic, beautiful, and colorful and felt very much like the Easter pageantry of Catholic services at St. Peter's Basilica in the Vatican.

On this night, everybody participating was styled either in Anglican robes or in African-inspired Episcopal wear. Some, however, were dressed by Macy's, Brooks Brothers, Saks Fifth Avenue, or their own tailored clothing. Everything, from the tall hat worn by the wife of the bishop-elect to the glittering, sparkling watches and arm bracelets, was quite beautiful to behold. The high-heeled shoes, the perfect hairdos, and the manicured nails all spoke to the importance of this event and the fact that Black folk have a style of their own, a way with the aesthetics of life that transcend economic and social status. In church, almost everybody looks economically well off and socially acceptable. From the outward appearance, everybody also looked like they had a job, a full-time way of earning a living, though I knew better.

The look of prosperity is a façade that characterizes the Black church from one Sunday to another. But nobody, no group or organization, can hold a candle to Black church folk and the way they dress on Sunday morning. Martha Nussbaum says that "style itself makes its claims, expresses its own sense of what matters. Literary form is not separable from philosophical content, but is, itself, a part of content—an integral part, then, of the search for and the statement of truth."[8] Now, that is the truth!

The consecration service was ultimately about truth wrapped up in style—the truth of the gospel, the truth of the call to preach, the truth of the word, and the search for a higher truth about life and justice. It was also about the meaning of Black faith, Black love, and the quest for freedom. Style makes truth easier to swallow and certainly easier to hear or listen to as sermonic discourse. This applies to Black preaching more than anything else. Preaching style seems to be what matters most to Black church folk. Do not misunderstand me here, because I believe that style as an element of aesthetics is important, and it is not an isolated phenomenon. It means something. And we all need a little pizzazz in delivering the sermonic message. It seems that pizzazz makes the preached word more palatable, and without it, you become a boring lecturer to most Black folk. This only applies to what congregations expect from Black preachers. Substance, style, and method in preaching are not all equal, and the slackers seldom slack on style, while substance and method are permanently banished from the pulpit—or if not banished, at least on sabbatical.

Now, back to the story. On that particular night, I wanted to be critical of the consecration event—lovingly critical, because I cannot escape criticism of self and other—but the spiritual nature of the worship service coupled with the words, the colors, the music, and the shouts were all quite beautiful and moving. There was a beauty seen in the faces and the entire bodies of throngs of Black folk coming together to elevate a young Black man to the office of bishop, to serve among the people in the community and in the Pentecostal church. I'm so glad that I can still recognize beauty and know it when I see it and when I hear it.

What I mean here is that the Black body is beautiful—shapely and statuesque. The mind is sharp too. The Black voice is even more beautiful, whether it is Hezekiah Walker, Shirley Caesar, Whitney Houston,

---

8. Martha Nussbaum, *Love's Knowledge: Essays on Philosophy and Literature* (New York: Oxford University Press, 1990), 3.

Aretha Franklin, Marvin Gaye, or Jessye Norman. And I dare not forget the voices of preachers like William A. Jones, Gardner Taylor, Samuel DeWitt Proctor, Bishop Gilbert E. Patterson, Martin Luther King Jr., and Fannie Lou Hamer. Black is beautiful!

Very little in my life can compare with worship on Easter Sunday in the Black church, or on any Sunday where a host of people are styling and smiling. Where the laughter is loud and boisterous, and where the music is smooth and jazzy, bluesy and full of fervor. But most of all, where the voice of the preacher and the power of the sermon creates new life, new hope, new dreams, and a new determination to keep on keeping on, just a little while longer, believing that everything will be all right, even in the face of somber and oppressive conditions of hate and evil. The sermon, uttered by the eloquent and sweet voice of the preacher, gives hope to those thousands who have been banished to the ash heaps of hopelessness and despair. The sermon is an instrument of creativity.

The Black preacher has historically embodied the claim of philosophers like Martha Nussbaum and Friedrich Nietzsche that form and content go together. Style or form is not simply decorative but substantive and determinative. The nexus between form and content cannot be disentangled. I am suggesting here that in order for the message of the preacher to be heard, it must be delivered in a way that facilitates the engagement of the hearer or reader. It cannot be as bland as a bowl of chicken broth. It needs a little bit of sugar and spice, a little leaven, a little sprinkling of salt and pepper. A little poetic flair. A little aestheticism. A little style and a touch of something that makes the congregation feel and believe that the preacher is indeed "one of us," creating a univocal spirit in the church.

Now, some preachers today indeed take it a bit too far and focus only on stylistics at the expense of content, without realizing or understanding that they must go hand in hand from start to finish. That is the poetics and aesthetics of speaking and writing out loud that I'm talking about, ones that more often than not seem to engulf and capture the Black church experience. The sermon should be an amalgamation of form and substance. It should be a masterful mixture of the two, so much so that their integration masks the clear delineation of one from the other. It is a hybridized representation of a dominant trope in Black life where on Sunday morning, the imbrication of middle class and poor, lettered and unlettered is blurred to the point of univocity—obliterating stratification on every discernable level. To the outsider peeping through the stained-glass windows of the church, Black faith looks like a smooth, flowing stream of righteousness and peace, speckled with shouts of praise and shrieks of unspeakable joy. It is a deeply engrained spirituality honed at the edge of suffering and death first encountered during the Middle Passage and the long nights of bondage, where the daylight of freedom took forever to show its hidden face.

Still, the preacher has to work hard at becoming a poet. This takes a lot of reading, re-reading, un-reading, writing, and re-writing. Also, study must be coupled with prayer and meditation if the preacher wants to be the embodiment of the word of God and the symbol of the Holy Spirit.

The Divine Word—The Poetry and the Prophecy

Comfort, O comfort my people says your God. [...] A voice says, "Cry out!" And I said, "What shall I cry?" All people are grass, their constancy is like the flower of the field. The grass withers, the flower fades, when the breath of the LORD blows upon it; surely the people are grass. The grass withers, the flower fades; but the word of God will stand forever.

—Isaiah 40:1, 6-8 (NRSV)

These majestic, marvelous, almost magical opening poetic words to this fortieth chapter of Isaiah ring resoundingly right to the top tier of our tortured and tattered personal and communal lives. The prophetic preacher is a poet in the pulpit. "Comfort, O comfort my people, says your God. Speak tenderly to Jerusalem, and cry to her that she has served her term, that her penalty is paid" (v. 2 NRSV). This is a decisive turning point in the lives of a broken and humiliated people. The debt that cut them off from God had been paid. A nation caught in the grip of their Babylonian captors, surrounded by the splash and splendor of all the gods of Babylon, wondered whether their God was powerful enough to defeat enemies, whether the glory of the Lord could make itself felt in the presence of emperors and armies. These people were no doubt thinking that God had forgotten all about them. That the grace of God had escaped them, that their troubles were everlasting, unending, and continuous. To these very people, a broken people on the brink of hopelessness and despair, who felt dejected and abandoned, a word of divine comfort unfolds.

Today, as African Americans—as Black men and women—we too feel the pinch and the pain of life's troubles. We feel like we are in our own Babylon and we wonder why. Why so much oppression and so much injustice? We feel like the lost searching soul of James Baldwin in *The Fire Next Time*. Nobody wants to even talk about history and slavery—American chattel slavery is like a myth. Many Blacks feel the same way, unwilling to recognize the searing impact of slavery and racism upon the social, psychological, and economic life of Black people, regardless of education, church affiliation, or social status. But this is a part of what is necessary to get in front of the text. We need to hear from the divine counsel this day. "Comfort, O comfort my people, says your God. Speak tenderly...and cry to her that she has served her term, that her penalty is paid."

Then the text points out the meaning of the imminent unfolding of the kingdom of God by showing that the glory of the Lord will be recognized by all people. The coming presence of the Lord will shake things up like never before.

> A voice cries out: "In the wilderness prepare the way of the LORD, make straight in the desert a highway for our God. Every valley shall be lifted up, and every mountain and hill be made low; the uneven ground shall become level, and the rough places a plain. Then the glory of the LORD shall be revealed, and all people shall see it together, for the mouth of the LORD has spoken." (Isa 40:3-5 NRSV)

Herein lies the meaning of transformation and revelation. The spiritual, topographic, and psychic landscape will be transformed. The wilderness, the church, and the city will be prepared and made ready. The wilderness will be reconstructed. The wilderness will be changed. This wilderness is not necessarily geographical; it is not simply the area that separates Babylon from Judah. This is also a metaphor for where God

59

dwells—where the Lord comes to rescue us from our fleeting and faltering hope. The Lord's appearing will make that which is uninhabitable fit for habitation. The power of the presence of God is such that the literal and figural desert that is unfit for travel will have a highway like Interstate 95 running right through it. The impossible will become possible, and the glory of the Lord will be revealed. The shrouded dimness of the present will be illumined by the glory of the Lord. The glory of the Lord shall be revealed—and not just to Jerusalem. Not just to Israel, not just to the prophet Isaiah or even those in the divine counsel. Not just to the few, but to the many. The text says that "All the people shall see it together, for the mouth of the LORD has spoken" (v. 5). Glory, Glory-hallelujah.

My beloved, this divine word is forever. It is everlasting, infinite, eternal, and enduring. This word, this divine word will withstand the ravaging destruction of war and all of our proclamations and declarations, our constitutions and amendments, our Supreme Court decisions and acts of US Congress. None can outlast God's divine word. A voice says, "Cry out!" And I said, "What shall I cry?" All people are grass, their constancy is like the flower of the field. The grass withers, the flower fades when the breath of the LORD blows upon it; surely the people are grass. The grass withers, the flower fades; but the word of our God will stand forever" (v. 6-8 NRSV). Yes, Pastor, be resolved to keep preaching God's word.

Yes, it is the message, not the messenger—that is, not the preacher—that matters. We are preaching the message! The message is the word of God. Do not be mad at the preacher for what the word of God says. Do not cop an attitude because of the preacher. It is not me; it is the word. As the preacher of the word, I do not have anything to say to you on my own—by myself. When I stand up to preach on Sunday morning, I'm trying with every fiber and ounce of energy in my mind and body to seriously explain and clearly expound upon God's word. It is not my word, but God's word. The preacher needs to teach people in no uncertain terms, saying, for example, "You may not like some things about me. I may be too dark complexioned for some, too short for others, and too heavy for some others. I may be a lot of things and fall short on a lot of occasions.

Accuse me of whatever you want, but I pray by the power of the Holy Spirit that you will not be able to accuse me of not staying in the word."

The word says clearly that "all people are grass." Not some, but all. Not the poor, but the rich and the poor. Not the homeless and the hungry, but all people are grass. Not only those who live in the ghetto, but also those who live on the riverfront on the bluff or high on top of the hill. Not just those who sweep the floors and collect the garbage, but those who own the building and refine the oil and make the wine and design the clothes and the cars. All flesh is grass. There is no distinction between the powerful and the powerless. No distinction between the rich and the poor, no distinction between the wise and the foolish, those who drive Bentleys and Ferraris and those who ride the city bus. All human beings stand on equal footing as "grass." The poetry is compelling. The language is lucid and lively. The language is jolting and electrifying, like a bolt of lightning.

Human life itself is fleeting, flawed by the futile and feckless nature of the flesh. All flesh is grass. As human beings, we are withered and wilted, wrangled and wrought by the radiant heat of life's searing and scorching arrows. Yes, we are withered by the worries that engulf us. We're worried about money. Withered. Worried about our health, our children, our youth. Withered. The grass withers, the flower fades, but the *word of our God* will stand forever. Everything else is temporary. Everything else is transitory. Everything else is momentary. Even life itself in all of its beauty is fleeting and faltering, but *God's word* will stand forever. Jesus says, "Heaven and earth will pass away, but *my words* will certainly not pass away" (Matt 24:35, emphasis added). This word is divine.

- Thy word have I hid in mine heart, that I might not sin against thee. (Ps 119:11 KJV)

- In the beginning was the Word and the Word was with God and the Word was God. (John 1:1)

- Thy word is a lamp unto my feet, and a light unto my path. (Ps 119:105 KJV)

The Poetic Flair of Seeing and Preaching the Word

The word that Isaiah son of Amoz saw concerning Judah and Jerusalem. [...]
For out of Zion shall go forth instruction, and the word
of the LORD from Jerusalem.
He shall judge between the nations, and shall arbitrate for many peoples;
they shall beat their swords into plowshares,
and their spears into pruning hooks;
nation shall not lift up sword against nation,
neither shall they learn war any more.

—Isaiah 2:1, 3-4 (NRSV)

The preacher as poet must be able to stand fearlessly and declare with fervor and flair the transforming word of God. This is a word that is against weapons of war and warlike behavior. It is a word about globalized prophesy, not localized hegemony. It is a word of hope, a word of cataclysmic transformation and peace. A word of power as picturesque as the mountaintop and as beautiful as the snowcapped hills of the Shenandoah, as curvaceous and as alive as the hills that lead to the top of the mountain at Jefferson's Monticello here in Virginia. This is the word. The powerful poetic word. The seen word. This is the word of God against the forces of evil and destruction.

In truth, this word of God is the preacher's opportunity to get in front of the text and preach the word of God against the powers of destruction. This is the word of God against the nuclear bomb, the F-16 fighter jet, the word of God against the submarine, the aircraft carrier. This is the word of God against the Imperium. This is the word of God staring empire, oppression, injustice, and evil right in the face. This is the naked word of God, the unencumbered prophetic word. The powerful word standing alone—yet surrounded by the admirals, the generals, and lieutenant commanders. The word of God speaking in defiance of military might and political power. The word of the God turning a deaf ear to the just-war theory and the "morality of laws" that continue to oppress and subjugate the Other. The word that the prophet Isaiah, the son of Amoz, saw.

The prophet *saw* the word. With his own eyes—he saw the word! The text does not say in this instance that he *heard* the word, but that he *saw* the word. Wow! When we speak, we do not see the words, but we hear them; but when God speaks to the prophet, God enables the prophet to see God's word, to understand and explain the word. This word is not a fleeting and faltering sound that fades into forgetfulness, but it is seen like the hovering of the clouds on the horizon of the storm. It is seen like the colors of the rainbow. The word, this word, is seen like the picture painted by the brush of a great artist like Vincent van Gogh or Pablo Picasso—or better yet like Jerome and Jeromyah Jones. This word is seen like the beautiful scenic landscapes that color the Earth in every corner of the globe—from ocean to ocean and sea to shining sea.

This word of God transcends Christian, Jewish, Islamic, and Marxist rhetoric as well as the posturing double-talk of American politics and democracy. This word is the word of truth. It needs little to no verifying. This word stands against the lie, against police officers in Cleveland who murdered Tamir Rice, a twelve-year-old Black boy. This word is against those police who murdered Laquan McDonald while he was running away from them. It is as clear to me as it was to Martin Luther King Jr. that war begets war. Weapons beget weapons, torture begets torture, and hate begets hate.

I know that there are some people who, for example, want to be more American than George Washington and Thomas Jefferson. But what will it take for the church, the Muslim temple, the synagogue, and people of God to realize that there is no end to war and violence? We have too many Black males killed, murdered either by another Black person or by the police—the symbol and force of the government. The police are the new slave masters. Autonomous and sovereign. These gun-toting, Clint Eastwood–like riflemen tend to shoot first and ask questions later when it comes to young Black males. This means that there is no counter-argument when a Black male or female is dead. You get one concocted narrative only—a narrative that not even the body camera or the cell phone camera can compete with. A fiction that boggles the mind. A Nobel Prize–winning narrative that is as false as it is ugly.

And yet the word is capable of transforming the Earth. Convulsing the Earth. "The nations will voluntarily renounce their arms, by forging their weapons into agricultural instruments" of peace.[9] Swords will be turned into plowshares, and spears into pruning hooks. This is not just eschatological talk; this is not just end-time visioning. This is now. This indeed is realized eschatology.[10] This is the eternal now.[11]

The word is the architect of creation. In the beginning was the word: "God said, 'Let there be light'" (Gen 1:3). Chaos was transformed into order by the power of the spoken word, the powerful word that has the ability to transform. Preach this same word, my brothers and sisters, in order to move communities forward and to transform both self and world. Be the poetic preacher that God has made you to be; speak wisdom, truth, love, and peace. Speak radical transformation. Speak in the spirit and language of the text: "He shall judge between the nations, and shall arbitrate for many peoples; they shall beat their swords into plowshares, and their spears into pruning hooks; nation shall not lift up sword against nation, neither shall they learn war any more" (Isa 2:4).

This is the poetic power of the transforming word, the preached word. The word of God is the final arbiter of disputes and disagreements. The word is a peace-producing word, a word that replenishes the Earth, plows the Earth, and enables it to yield the smells of life, the aromatic sprouts of spring and summer bringing forth new life every morning—not the blood of corruption and the destruction of war, not the fire and brimstone of Armageddon. This powerful word produces love and peace. No longer is there a need for weapons of war, weapons of mass destruction, car bombs and landmines, guns and battleships. No more tools and strategies of war. No more iron and steel designed to bring about death and destruction. The nations, the warriors, they shall beat their swords into plowshares, cultivating the earth, tilling up the soil, and turn their spears into pruning hooks, so that the vines can produce more fruit to feed the hungry and

9. Otto Kaiser, *Isaiah 1–12* (Philadelphia: Westminster, 1983), 28.

10. See Albert Schweitzer, *The Quest of the Historical Jesus* (Mineola, NY: Dover Publications, 2005).

11. See Paul Tillich, *The Eternal Now* (New York: Charles Scribner's Sons, 1963).

poor scattered across Africa, Asia, Europe, and America. That is what we want.

Preach poetically and transform the church. Transform the community. Transform the world. Use your own jazzy poetic flair to tap into the poetry of the word of God. For me, I see poetry everywhere in scripture—not rhyme, not symmetrical verse, not alliteration—but the spirit and depth of meaning and understanding. Listen and see the poetry of freedom and transformation in this scripture text from the fourth chapter of the Gospel of Luke:

> And he came to Nazareth, where he had been brought up; and he went to the synagogue, as his custom was, on the Sabbath day. And he stood up to read; and there was given to him the book of the prophet Isaiah. He opened the book and found the place where it was written. "The Spirit of the Lord is upon me, because he has anointed me to preach good news to the poor. He has sent me to proclaim release to the captives and recovering of sight to the blind, to set at liberty those who are oppressed, to proclaim the acceptable year of the Lord." And he closed the book, and gave it back to the attendant, and sat down; and the eyes of all in the synagogue were fixed on him. And he began to say to them, "Today this scripture has been fulfilled in your hearing." (Luke 4:16-21 NRSV)

This passage shows very clearly the value and consequences of prophetic ministry, which is exactly what Jesus was about. The power of the gospel is such that it not only heals, forgives, and frees the oppressed, whoever and wherever they are, but it also causes and creates conflict because of its truth. Conflict is often a prelude to understanding the gospel. Conflict fosters resistance by those who think of themselves as privileged, like those in the text who felt that they were more privileged than the Gentiles. Notice the transforming social nature of his poetic message: Jesus was chosen to take the good news to the poor, to those who do not have very much, who have been economically deprived. Those at the bottom of the well and at the bottom of the barrel will have good news brought to them.

Even as Jesus was sent to "proclaim release to the captives" (or translated from Isaiah 58:6 NRSV, "to let the oppressed go free"), the preacher as poet must do the same. That is what the gospel is about! It is about releasing folk from guilt, from debts—from whatever is being held over their head! It is about forgiveness, wiping the slate clean, never to hold it against a person again! We cannot go wrong if we ground our forward preaching and our teaching in the word of God by seeking to "set at liberty those who are oppressed."

To let the oppressed go free—to liberate the oppressed. Those who are treated with disdain and dejection, the oppressed. Those who are subjected to evil acts of violence because of their race or gender, the oppressed. Those who suffer from the vengeful ravages of a racist society. Those who are treated like Jefferson in Ernest Gaines's novel *A Lesson Before Dying*. Those who are called hogs or animals. Those who are wrongfully accused by a system that is stacked against them shall one day walk in freedom, the oppressed. Those who have suffered from having their dignity snatched and stolen from them by the architects of racism and injustice. The oppressed shall be set free, liberated by the gospel of Jesus Christ.

This text from Luke and Isaiah is, to me, is the epitome of the poetic. And the preacher is called to make this pivotal text outlining liberation and transformation as plain as possible. I'm not preaching, but I'm teaching preaching by trying to get in front of the text. And as a poet, the preacher is called and compelled to "do things" with words and to bring out the inherent poetry that resides in the word. This poetry is itself a type of getting in front of the text.

After Jesus had given his proclamation, he rolled up the scroll, gave it back to the attendant, and sat down. How aesthetic. How powerfully poetic. How dramatic and stylistic. And he said to them, "Today, this scripture has been fulfilled in your hearing" (Luke 4:21 NRSV). Allow me to get in front of this text:

> Today, in your very presence, the reign of God has arrived; today, the kingdom is being realized in your very midst; today, the present and the future have joined hands and past prophecy has come to light. Today, the revelation of God has been fully and faithfully revealed; today, the message of the messiah has been heralded and heard. Today, the meaning of the gospel has been shared, explained, and understood. Today, the good news has arrived;

today, time and eternity have joined hands in holy matrimony and shall be bound together from this day forward. Today, realized eschatology has taken form, and infinity and totality have been glimpsed in the temple of the Almighty God.

Today, whatever was will never be again. Today, nihilism has died and hope has been resurrected—reborn, rejuvenated, and rekindled. Today, we shall see things differently than we saw them in the past because today transformation has taken place. Today, the poor and the homeless will be looked after; today, the guilty will be declared innocent; today, the accused shall be forgiven. Today, the preacher and the church have been given new life; today, the church has been given new direction, new hope, and new spiritual power. Today, we can get in front of the text and allow this text to transform us into preachers unashamed to declare God's word.

It is now—right now, right here. Today, not yesterday; today, not last year; today, not last week, not even tomorrow or next week, but today! Today, not someday; today, not another day, not another time, not another place, but today, this scripture has been fulfilled in your hearing. There is no waiting period. There is no period of preparation, no more getting ready, no more anticipation, no more speculation. But today! Jesus has already done it. The fulfillment and hope, the revelation and transformation have come!

If you are poor, today is your day for transformation. If you are blind physically or spiritually, today is your day. If you have always been a liar, a cheat, a drug addict, a sinner, a backslider, a "this or a that," I have come in the spirit of the poet and prophet to say unto you that, today, forgiveness has arrived, and you have been forgiven for all your past transgressions, missteps, and shortcomings. Hold your head up and realize that every time you breathe, that every breath you take is an instantiation of the creative power of God making you all over again! Today is your day for healing, today is your day for hope, today is your day for redemption, and today is your day for transformation. I can do things today that I could not do yesterday because today is a new day! Today, by the anointing of the Holy Spirit, this scripture has been fulfilled in your hearing.

67

JONAH IV: "From Defiance to Deliverance"

*As my life was ebbing away, I remembered the LORD; and my prayer came to you,
into your holy temple. Those who worship vain idols forsake their true loyalty.
But I with the voice of thanksgiving will sacrifice to you;
what I have vowed I will pay. Deliverance belongs to the LORD!*

—Jonah 2:7-9 (NRSV)

Life in general has been very tough for me and for a host of Black folk who have any semblance of consciousness and understanding about the two Americas we live in—fifty-five years after the passing of the Civil Rights Act of 1964 and sixty years after Brown v. Board of Education of Topeka. The policeman who shot the eighteen-year-old Black boy Trayvon Martin has supporters who have raised nearly a half million dollars for his defense. Now, we know that some of our Black youth are not without some fault and some guilt. But that does not justify these trigger-happy cops shooting down our Black boys like they are dogs. When I think about that, they may even be treated worse than dogs.

The results of a Pew Research Foundation[12] survey said most Black folk believe that racism is alive and well in Ferguson, Missouri, and Richmond, Virginia, and every other area that has Black and white folk. Conversely, almost all the white folk surveyed said that the police were justified and anything done to Black people is okay. It is time that Black people everywhere stand up against this Wild West mentality toward Black women and men in America.

Yes, the young and old of St. Louis and its suburbs have been defiant in not sitting back, acting satisfied with injustice and blatant acts of disrespect and disregard for Black life. I am troubled by this continued hatred toward the Black body. Black males are the most hated, the most reviled, the most suspect, the most despised human beings in America and around the world. This reality causes mental stress and physical disease, such as heart disease, diabetes, high blood pressure, and high cholesterol.

12. See Anna Brown, "Key Findings on Americans' Views on Race in 2019," survey, Washington, DC; The Pew Research Center and John Gramlich, "From Police to Parole, Black and White Americans Differ Widely in Their Criminal Justice System," survey, Washington, DC, The Pew Research Center, 2019.

It causes high drop-out rates, drug use, and pleasure seeking through sex, weed smoking, partying, drinking, and a host of other negative activities.

Yes, our people need to be educated, trained, and encouraged. Our boys and girls need to be tutored in reading and math, history and literature. They need to be loved, not denigrated and killed. They need to be encouraged, not talked about and called *thugs,* a word that the Miami Police Union President and three St. Louis police officers used in reference to Tamir Rice and Michael Brown, respectively.[13] He has not indicted the police officer who killed the Black teenager because he thinks of Black males as thugs. And how can a grand jury of a majority Black town be made up of 75 percent white and 25 percent Black? This is still a tragedy and travesty in this year and time.

Jonah has been through some stuff and much of it was his own doing. He has been disobedient and defiant. And some of our Black males have been the same way, going in the wrong direction, doing the wrong things, hanging out with their "homies," who are doing stupid and silly stuff. That is what we see happened in the movie the day before the young man was to start college at the University of Oregon.

Now, in our text, Jonah is praying. He has gotten himself in a whole heap of trouble trying to escape the presence of the Lord. But he cannot get away. The text says, "As my life was ebbing away, I remembered the Lord; and my prayer came to you, into your holy temple" (2:7 NRSV).

Listen, no matter how defiant we have been, no matter how determined we are to do what we want to do and to act like God is not God, we cannot escape our own memory of the Lord. Things do fall apart. And our lives fall apart. We fall from grace. We fall off the wagon. Our lives ebb (fall) away, and we too remember the Lord. When we are faced with the crossroads of life, when we are caught in the quagmire of hopelessness,

13. See Tim Elfrink, Miami Police Union President on Tamir Rice: "Act Like a Thug and You'll Be Treated Like One," *Miami New Times,* December 30, 2015, accessed August 6, 2019, https://www.miaminewtimes.com/news/miami-police-union-president-on-tamir-rice-act-like-a-thug-and-youll-be-treated-like-one-8141523; Conor Friedersdorf, Sadism in the St. Louis Police Department: "Three cops who expressed an eagerness to brutalize protesters unintentionally targeted the one person likely to get them arrested," *The Atlantic,* December 3, 2018, accessed August 6, 2019, https://www.theatlantic.com/ideas/archive/2018/12/st-louis-police-brutality-stockley/577174

despair, and death, we still have the wherewithal to remember the Lord. We have an anamnestic consciousness that engulfs us.

Jonah was struggling with holding onto his life, trying to survive sloshing around in the entrails of the fish, and he remembered the Lord. Beloved, do you not remember what the Lord has done for you today? How the Lord brought you up from the push and pull of trying to survive? How the Lord enabled you to get a job when it seemed like you were not going to make it? How the Lord sent an angel to help you feed your family; how the Lord got you to the doctor, to the hospital just in the nick of time; how the Lord provided a fish to help you along the way? This fish is a metaphor for a friend: a lawyer, a doctor, a pastor, a teacher.

Jonah seemed to be almost gone, almost lost to the chilly hands of death, almost drowning and suffocating in the belly of this large fish. But he remembers and we can see now how his defiance has turned into deliverance. Jonah says, "I remembered the LORD; and my prayer came to you, into your holy temple. Those who worship vain idols forsake their true loyalty. But I with the voice of thanksgiving will sacrifice to you; what I have vowed, I will pay. Deliverance belongs to the LORD" (v. 7-9).

Yes, yes! God is our deliverer. Deliverance belongs to the Lord. I know that some of us are quite ego-driven, and some of us think that we can do it on our own. But rest assured that you cannot deliver yourself. "Who will rescue me from this body of death?" (Rom 7:24 NRSV). In the final analysis, our defiance gives way to deliverance because we recognize that our own weakness and frailty is not sufficient. Only God's sufficiency can transform defiance into deliverance. Amen.

UN-READING

From Sermon to Social Action

JONAH V: "Misplaced Anger"

> *When God saw what they did, how they turned from their evil ways, God changed his mind about the calamity that he had said he would bring upon them; and he did not do it.*

—Jonah 3:10 (NRSV)

> *But this was very displeasing to Jonah and he became angry [...]*
> *And the LORD said, "Is it right for you to be angry?"*

—Jonah 4:1, 4 (NRSV)

Un-reading means resistance to a dominant traditional reading that subjugates the voices of the marginalized. Jesus un-reads the familiar text in his time. Jesus's parables are good examples: For example, leaven (Matt 13:33), mustard seed (Luke 13:20-21), vineyard workers (Matt 20:1-16), and Father and two sons (Matt 21:28-32). Society reads the text in a certain way, but Jesus *un-reads* (reverses) it, forging a new meaning.[1]

By definition, "a parable is a story cast alongside of life for the sake of leading the audience to see something differently."[2] C. H. Dodd also defines *parable* similarly:

---

1.   See Dr. Yung Suk Kim, *Jesus's Truth: Life in Parables* (Lanham, MD: Lexington Books, forthcoming).

2.   Marcus Borg, *Jesus: The Life, Teaching, and Relevance of a Religious Revolutionary* (New York: HarperCollins, 2008), 259.

At its simplest the parable is a metaphor or simile drawn from nature or common life, arresting the hearer by its vividness or strangeness, and leaving the mind in sufficient doubt about its precise application to tease it into active thought."[3]

We modern readers also must un-read certain texts in the New Testament. Among others, some of the post-Pauline texts may be good cases that involve repressive social relations, which are expressed with the so-called "household codes" that regulate various household relationships between master and slave, husband and wife, and parents and children. Women's subordinate position in 1 Timothy 2:11-15 is also a good case. In all of these household codes or women-degradation texts, one has to read, re-read, and un-read because the ultimate meaning is not controlled by the past or by any authorities today. Meaning or interpretation is a politically self-conscious business in which one has to take a stance. Namely, abusive or sexist texts should be named and rejected. In the stages of reading and re-reading, one has to ask why these seemingly unnecessary texts for today's readers are there in the early church. This process will help readers to see what happened in the past and to engage us in critical contexts then and now.

The other text in mind is 1 Corinthians 14:33b-36, which is considered interpolation, meaning an inserted text by the later editor of the church, possibly long after Paul's death (as we see similar kind of texts in 1 Tim 2:11-15). Except for this particular passage in 1 Corinthians, Paul's overall letters (meaning his undisputed letters, seven in total) do not have women-degradation passages. Rather, the opposite is the case: Paul calls women apostles (Rom 16:7), and Galatians 3:28 is radical in terms of gender relations. So readers have to un-read 1 Corinthians 14:33b-36 because it is not Paul's voice or theology. And, even if it were his voice, the texts demand an un-reading!

When it comes to the Gospels, Mark 9:1 will be a different case that readers have to read, re-read, un-read, and tell their positions. While some consider it as Jesus's own saying, others render it a Markan addition or creation. In either case, readers have to struggle to understand what it means to hear this apocalyptic saying in the first century CE and now.

---

3. C. H. Dodd, *The Parables of the Kingdom* (New York: Scribner, 1961), 5.

Eventually, one must decide about this text and interpret it for today's world by un-reading all previous interpretations. I think this text is more technical in nature, so it may not be easy to come to a conclusion.

In our text, Jonah is burning mad, burning with anger because God has been merciful and gracious to Nineveh, rather than allowing the great city to be destroyed like he said he would. God has shown that God is a repentant and reflective God, one whose mind can be changed if the people turn from their evil ways. It is the goodness of God that trips up Jonah and causes him to show his backside, his hind parts, his gluteus maximus. Jonah is so mad at God that he has the nerve to sit in judgment of God. He is trying to judge the judge of the universe. His anger is misplaced.

His anger then leads to a very hateful prayer. It is almost funny or comedic, if not tragic, because Jonah sounds like a spoiled child, like a little boy who is mad because his brother has done something to deserve a "whipping," but the father, instead of following through on promised punishment, changes his mind. Instead of punishing him, he hugs him or buys him a toy or some ice cream, and the other brother gets mad because his brother did not receive a whipping as promised. That is the way often we are. Too often we are mad. Our anger is out of place—not simply because of what God has done for someone else, but some of us are just quick to get angry over the smallest, most insignificant thing.

Listen up, Black, brown, and white people. Our people, our youth, and their friends are always in the paper or on the news for committing some act of violence against one another, oftentimes for something as absurd as stepping on someone's tennis shoes, looking at someone's girl the wrong way, or "disrespecting" other family members. So the banality of anger that we see too often in the Black community, in the Black family, and in the Black church is misplaced. Do not be mad at your mama and grandma because they do not allow you to bring contraband in the house or because they insist on your going to school and doing your homework, or that they insist on turning off the TV and spending some time reading and studying instead of playing games. Do not be mad about that. Do not be mad because somebody has a job that pays more than yours or because your friends are living better, eating better, dressing better, and looking like they are doing better than you. That is no reason for you to be mad and display an ugly attitude.

Our anger is misplaced when we display behaviors that are self-destructive and destructive toward those who look just like you. Those whose face is the mirror image of our own. Do not get so angry with your teachers and counselors that you stop going to school. Your failure and dropping out of school only hurts you and your family—not those you are angry with. If you get so angry and harm somebody else by committing a crime, you are hurting yourself as well as others, but you are not doing anything to address the system's biases and injustices toward poor people, Black people, or people who are in your same social, economic, and political situation.

Let us not do to ourselves and each other that which is harmful. If you are going to be angry, make sure it is justified. Make sure it is based on some type of unrighteousness and injustice or mistreatment of God's people, not misplaced anger based on ego and self-righteousness.

But what exactly is misplaced anger? Misplaced anger is unjustified anger. It has no basis in anything but our own ego, our own bruised self. Jonah is mad because of God's goodness, and God's ability to be God makes Jonah's prophecy suspect because God is not restrained by what God said before. God is not simply a God who directs his prophets, but God also lets them know when to cut out some of their foolishness and evil. God asks Jonah, "Who gave you the right to be angry?" We have no right to be angry because God has been good to somebody else. God can bless, forgive, and show mercy to whomever God desires. And all of us have been recipients of love and grace.

Getting in Front of the Text

But her brain was not interested in the future.

—Toni Morrison, *Beloved*

Finally, brethren, whatsoever things are true, whatsoever things are honest, whatsoever things are just, whatsoever things are pure, whatsoever things are lovely, whatsoever things are of good report; if there be any virtue, and if there be any praise, think on these things.

—Philippians 4:8 (KJV)

Preachers have to learn to live in eternity, while in the midst of time.

—Samuel DeWitt Proctor

We are called upon to wrestle with the great idea.

—Howard Thurman

The text is an action, and the word *action* means to be propelled forward in a certain spiritual and physical sense. So, getting in front of the text means moving forward in a new and transformative way. Furthermore, this means that at some point, sooner rather than later, the preacher has to move from the high and lofty elevation of the pulpit podium to the level of the street, where the words of the scripture text and the sermon itself become embodied in the life and actions of the preacher and the people. The sermon is not simply a verbalized mental construct. The sermon is not an ordinary speech to be spoken and then forgotten, but it must rise up from the page and create powerful, transformative action. The sermon must always *do something*. The words of the sermon must be compelled to inspire in the preacher and in the people a desire to do, to act—to become not just a hearer, but a doer of the word (James 1:22). An active participant in making the meaning of the word, God's word, come alive is like a spark of fire or an electric current that can shock the dying body and soul back to life. The word is a transforming and life-giving force.

When the word happens, the action itself is not only the embodiment of the scripture text, but the action becomes an eventful corollary text—this new text is representative of the word of God, that is, the gospel in creative transformative action. The gospel or good news is not meant to be limited to words or writing and speaking or preaching. The logos is also an action. A sharp, bold, and blatantly unforgettable action. It is the ultimate creative action. The action of the preacher and his or her words is now itself a text—not just the performance of the existing scripture text, but a newly created text born out of struggle, hope, and the power of the Holy Spirit, resulting in transformative social action. Not just concern for the poor, but action on behalf of the poor and oppressed.

Jesus's words in Luke 4, "The Spirit of the Lord is upon me," suggest that the mysterious, magisterial, meaningful language and word is grounded in the power of the preached word and the Holy Spirit, which creates and necessitates action. The sermon that does not leave the pulpit is a wanton and worthless wrangling of feckless, earthly words. It is, in fact, an affront to God and the Holy Spirit. It is the antithesis of serious sermonic discourse.

Many of our ancestors, who could not read or write because they were forbidden by law and custom right here in Virginia and throughout the South, often said they'd rather "see a sermon than hear one." They had heard enough gibberish masquerading as a sermon spewed forth from the mouth of the slave master. Seeing the sermon is the action of the sermon manifested in doing something, like setting the captives free and feeding the poor. Like helping young people graduate from high school and college, advocating for the elevation of the poor and oppressed, and fighting against illiteracy, injustice, and the pipeline to prison, which seems to engulf and incinerate the hopes and dreams of too many Black children, youth, and adults.

From Getting in Front of the Text to Action that Transforms

My approach throughout this book is neither synchronic or diachronic, meaning that I am not too interested in the world within the text, nor the world behind the text. The social or political conditions that created the literary and contextual construction of the text are not my ultimate focus or concern, although they may be important. Rather, I contend that discovering and explaining the world in front of the text is the locus of transformation and liberation. Getting in front of the text is where we want to be, and it involves exploring "the world that the text creates."[4] This is so powerful and freeing because it allows for the love and grace of God to make a direct axis through one's life in a way that is not encumbered by the baggage of the past or the limitations of the present. It is the future and all that it promises, including the possible negation or

---

4. See Michael J. Gorman, *Elements of Biblical Exegesis* (Peabody, MA: Hendrickson, 2001), 17.

neutralizing of past transgressions and mistakes that allows one to rejoice and shout, "Hallelujah! Praise the Lord!"

The scripture text that gives rise to thought and action is the driver of the sermon.[5] It is not enough for the text to cause one to think, but the text must cause and compel one to act. To get up off your posterior, your gluteus maximus, and to actually do something. Understanding and explaining a text is not revealed by the so-called intentions of the author. The text often has inherent plurivocity, or multiplicity of meanings, that are not arbitrary, though they may seem to be at first glance. There is a surplus of meaning in every text, not just the meanings discovered by Thomas Aquinas, Martin Luther, John Calvin, and, I daresay, St. Augustine. Every interpretation is not equal, which means that some interpretations are not only inferior to others, but some are negatively "off the chain" and downright irrational or off-base and wrong ethically, socially, spiritually, and otherwise. Some interpretations are socially and theologically inept, racially offensive, and oppressive, especially if they do not speak to the physical, spiritual, and social needs of the community, particularly to those on the underside of culture. Meaning is influenced by context, time, and culture. Context changes. Time changes. Culture changes. Meaning changes.

Scripture is, unfortunately, too often used as a pretext for the preacher to say what he or she wants to say—apart from the meaning of the text. This is a problem that I observe over and over again among ministry students, preachers, and pastors. There has to be a commitment to the text that does not end in an adulterous promiscuity or what I call sermonic adultery or sermonic fornication. I think that the language of sexuality is appropriate here because it has a level of universality that the preacher and all elements of humanity can easily understand, mainly because it is inherently and grossly human—"All too human," to use the language of philosophers Friedrich Nietzsche and Hannah Arendt.[6] This is also the language of the Black Church that permeates my own experience.

---

5. Paul Ricoeur says that "the symbol gives rise to thought" in his book *The Symbolism of Evil*; however, as he moves from being a philosopher of symbols to one of texts, I have interpreted his focus on textuality to create the analogue stated above: "The text gives rise to thought."

6. See Friedrich Nietzsche, *Human, All Too Human* (New York: Prometheus Books, 2009).

There seems to be a proclivity to choose a text and then to abandon it for another text that may or may not be analogous to the chosen text. It appears to be inherent to the preacher's lack of commitment to textuality in sermon development. This is problematic because it scatters the preacher's thoughts all over the place and undermines every element of the sermon. Once the preacher abandons the chosen text for another text in the middle of the sermon, this means, in effect, that the title of the sermon has also been abandoned, and by implication, the sermon's proposition has been abandoned as well. I call this ubiquitous preaching practice *textual abandonment*.

For example, switching from John 3:16 to 1 Corinthians 13:12 changes the focus of the sermon from God's love of creation to creation's or humanity's lack of understanding of the meaning of love as a revolutionary and transformative act. The John 3:16 text, "God so loved the world that he gave his only Son, so that everyone who believes in him may not perish but will have eternal life," is theocentric to the core. But the 1 Corinthians text is grounded in a weak and fallible anthropology that makes a mockery of both agape love and erotic love. In one text, Christ is the center, but in the other, the focus is different. They have their own integrity apart from each other. So, as a rule, the preacher cannot be jumping from one text to another just because the texts sound alike, or seem to be related, or because it makes you look biblically literate and smart to those who do not seem to know any better. Let us rethink this because what it does is makes you look and sound like somebody who does not know the difference between theology, Christology, and anthropology. Stay focused on the chosen text and leave the other texts alone until another day and time—until another sermon.

Sermon Point Development— The Body of the Sermon

It seems to me that one of the difficulties faced by the preacher is to learn how to carve and craft "points" or "moves" from the chosen scripture text, the text that the sermon is based upon. The language of points has been used in African-American preaching for as long as I can remember; however, the language of moves is a recent phenomenon coined by David Buttrick in his book *Homiletic: Moves and Structures*.[7]

Notice now that I am a bit Freudian, that is, obsessed and fixated on insisting that the sermon be textual and not topical. My philosophy is that you do not have to be much of a preacher to talk about topics, though topical preaching has received lots of accolades and has quite a large following—maybe for that very reason. But it is my contention that biblical/scriptural/textual preaching has a greater chance of being transformative if it is grounded in a scriptural text and not in a topic that takes you from one text to another: "Turn to John 3:11. Now let us turn to Revelation 6:1. Now turn to Exodus 4:13, and now turn back to Genesis 1:16." You are tossing and turning throughout the sermon, unable and unwilling to commit yourself to the development of a particular and uniquely chosen text. Allow me to overstate the case in my own language. This is what I call textual abandonment. This is textual promiscuity. It is textual adultery. It is a form of infidelity. It is being completely unfaithful and uncommitted to the chosen text!

Preachers are compelled to try to get in front of the text. I recommend the following process as a prelude to sermon point development.

Identify the scripture passage. Start with a scripture text of your own choosing, or choose from the lectionary, or develop your own system for choosing a scripture from week to week, month to month, or year to year.

Explore passage from various translations. Spend a lot of time—hours and even days—reading, re-reading, un-reading, and studying the language or words of the chosen scripture text. By language, I mean the translated or untranslated text. You do not have to know Greek, Aramaic, Hebrew, German, or French. Translations are tricky and subjective; though naturally some translations are better than others and some offer different insights; however, all of them, in my view, must be approached with a healthy degree of suspicion, a hermeneutic of suspicion. I am culturally

---

7. David Buttrick, *Homiletic: Moves and Structures* (Philadelphia: Fortress, 1987).

and theologically suspicious of all biblical texts. And yet I love them all. My suspicion is a form of love.

Seek to understand. Study, learn, and seek to know the meaning of every word or phrase in the chosen scriptural text. If you are using a scripture text as the source of the sermon, then you, as the preacher, are bound by it, wedded to it, and compelled to wrestle with it until you have some modicum of understanding. Remember, you cannot explain any text that you do not understand. Understanding precedes explanation and certainly is a necessary precondition for preaching. Seek to understand the text so that you can explain it to yourself and others. This explanation inevitably will lead to a deeper understanding and application.

Commit the text to mind and memory. Write out the chosen text or pericope in the liturgical reading you prefer and practice memorization of the text. Write the text with your own hand as a way of making it resonate in your heart and soul. Then, translate or interpret the text in your own language. Put it in your own words.

At this point, you have come upon an understanding of the text and have in mind an angle to the sermon. You better understand the main emphasis of the scripture text as well as the auxiliary and ancillary foci of the text. You have deeply considered what the text means to you and how it might resonate with your particular congregation and broader community concerns, given your particular social context.

List sermon title options with your audience top in mind. Allow the semantic autonomy of the text, that is, your understanding of the meaning of the particular chosen text, to influence your sermon title. Sketch a list of potential sermon titles that reflect your interpretation of the passage and what it is trying to say to you and your people, given your social and cultural context. As you start, try to come up with not just one title, but five or six titles that will work Sunday morning. Write these titles down on a separate sheet of paper and put them aside for a day or so.

Choose a textual title. After brainstorming as many sermon titles as possible, seek to pare down your *textually suggested* titles. Every sermon only needs one title, which is the result of reading, re-reading, and un-reading. This one particular title should be the best of the list for now and should lend itself to clarity, simplicity, ease of understanding, and ease of explanation. The preacher needs to internalize the sermon title.

Mitigate mumbling. Remember, that as the preacher, you cannot explain what you do not understand! A scripture text needs to be understood by the preacher first. If you try to preach what you do not understand, you will fumble, mumble, tumble, and bumble along. Do not do a disservice to God, the people, and the gospel by being unprepared and unfocused. The only way to mitigate against that is to commit yourself to the practice of reading and studying the scripture. Prayer is a necessary ingredient in this entire process.

What is the big, relevant question that emerges from the text? The sermon should ask a relevant, meaningful, powerful, practical question that can be answered by the scripture text itself and your understanding and interpretation of that text. This question should be made obvious in the introduction of the sermon. And you should not ask a question that the scripture text cannot answer because folk are seeking answers to practical issues and problems, not theoretical and hypothetical musing about things that do not matter to the folk in the pews. The very moment you ask a question that is driven by something other than the scripture text, you have just set yourself up to travel down a road where your sermon will likely implode or fall apart or morph into something that you want to say, apart from the integrity of the scripture text. Remember that it is not about you in any ultimate sense. It is about the grace and love of God, which allows you as the preacher to get out in front of the text in order to transform the world.

The "three-point" sermon is not sacred. The body of the sermon will develop the main points that the preacher has extrapolated from the text. Let me say unequivocally that the point or points of the sermon are determined by the scripture text itself and the adeptness and creativity of the preacher—not by another text! This means that there is no such thing as "three points" unless the scripture text has in it three things that demand to be developed. There is nothing sacred about having three points when one, two, or four are called for by the chosen text. But all sermons should have at least one point! And it is better to have one well-developed and highly textual point than to try to manufacture three points out of a one-point scripture text.

Pay attention to both visceral and depth perception. The architecture of a sermon point is critical, and this is rather theoretical. I want to say a word about the complex interplay between two modes of perception—presentational immediacy and causal efficacy. Actually, this interplay is termed symbolic reference.[8] In developing a point, the preacher should focus on the immediacy or epidermal nature of the point based on the text. In other words, presentational immediacy is what "jumps out" at you on a very visceral level as you read, re-read, un-read, and extrapolate a point from the chosen text. This extrapolation may lack sufficient depth and sophistication, but it is worthy of attention and will need more development and depth. This sermonic depth is what I am calling *causal efficacy*. This is moving from scratching the surface, or saying what is obvious to the average reader, to digging for a deeper meaning using all your resources.

Both approaches—the visceral and digging deeper for effectiveness—make the scripture text come alive in the real lives of real people. When people testify that God healed them from a disease or delivered them from an addiction, they mean this in a tangible way—not healing as a metaphor, but healing as an experience, a transformation from sickness to wellness, from weakness to strength, from faithlessness to faithfulness.

The Word of God: Sharper Than a Two-Edged Sword

Preaching strong, well-developed sermons that are tightly constructed is a difficult and continuous process that requires a broad understanding and love of people, knowledge of the biblical text, and awareness of the social and spiritual concerns and needs of the particular congregation. Social context is a necessary ingredient in hermeneutics and homiletics. In addition to these basic requirements, there is the need to know why

---

8. See Alfred North Whitehead, *Process and Reality* (New York: Free Press, 1978). The concept of symbolic reference in the language of Whitehead is akin to Paul Ricoeur's ostensive reference.

and what to do in order to put together a sermon that speaks to the heart and soul of folk who come to church week after week in order to "hear a word" from the Lord via the preacher and the sermon. And they expect this sermon to change their lives in some inexplicable way.

This is really a miracle and a mystery in an age of social, cultural, political, and technological change, in an age of Twitter, Facebook, Snapchat, and Instagram. In an age of addiction to the cell phone and addiction to pleasure and feel good desires twenty four hours a day sustained and fueled by toxic substances that have become cravings like the fructose in everything we eat and the caffeine in everything we drink and the opioids we feed ourselves as if they were Vitamin C or Vitamin D. This is an awesome responsibility for which none of us has been adequately prepared; however, I endeavor to outline the process of sermon development and then demonstrate that process and method for you as much as possible. I know that the preaching teacher does not have the luxury of being as completely theoretical as some historians, philosophers, and theologians. I say this because the sermon itself is the best speaker and demonstrator of the spiritual and reasonable nature of the homiletical task. It must be your best work at all times.

Preaching remains the heart and soul of the Black church, as Cleo LaRue and Henry Mitchell have explained,[9] and the metaphor of the sermon as a two-edged sword represents, for me, the value and importance of dialectic textual preaching and the effort to get in front of the text. Preaching does indeed cut both ways. By this, I mean that the real and the ideal are brought together. One edge is construed as the thesis, or the ideal, as seen in the scripture text, and the other edge of the same sword is the antithesis, or the real-life situation. Together, in terms of preaching method, they constitute the introduction of the sermon, which is often grounded in negativity, but not absolutely.

In simple dialectical terms, the real creates a tension represented in the life we all live—where good and evil, right and wrong, justice and injustice, joy and sorrow, pain and pleasure, and love and hate have to be negotiated and mediated every day in the physical body, in the social

---

9. See for example Cleophus LaRue, *The Heart of Black Preaching* (Louisville: Westminster John Knox, 2000), and Henry Mitchell, *Black Preaching* (Nashville: Abingdon Press, 1990).

community, and in the world. The book of James makes this clear when it asserts that out of the same mouth comes blessing and cursing (James 3:10). Similarly, the book of Hebrews says,

> God's word is living, active, and sharper than any two-edged sword. It penetrates to the point that it separates the soul from the spirit and the joints from the marrow. It's able to judge the heart's thoughts and intentions. (4:12)

The antithesis would postulate that, according to the text above, we live in a word-infested world. These words in the real world, in the tough and tumble of real life are not always alive and active, nor sharp, encouraging, and enlightening. They are sometimes dim and dull, empty and envious, encircling our experiences of joy with ugly expressions of enmity, evil, and hate. The words that people use, the things that we say to others and what is said to us, about us, and by us can do good or harm. Words can build up or tear down. Words can create hope and love, or they can cause fear and despair. Some words written, spoken, read, or heard are plain ugly and mean. Others are creative and life-giving.

Un-reading the Preaching Self and Other as Texts

As a pastor and preaching teacher, I lovingly try to build up the preacher's confidence and efforts, but some fluff that the preacher puts forth posing as a sermon is, in fact, a mess and must be discouraged and disallowed with my carefully chosen words. As a preacher and homiletics professor, I encourage you today to refrain from saying that another preacher such demeaning and derogatory words as this fellow preacher called by God "cannot preach." Think about what those words mean and think about how debilitating and destructive those words are. And ask yourself, "How did I become the judge of whether a person can preach or not?" Even a homiletics professor should be careful in making such judgments.

Further, what do you mean when you say such words? Are you talking about the architecture of the sermon or the methodology used in the construction of the sermon, or are you talking about the lack of correlation between the scripture text and the sermon's title? Are you talking about the language and logic of the sermon? Are you talking about the diachronic or synchronic message of the sermon? But most likely, you are making a judgment about the preacher's style, antics, or orality. Is your criticism regarding the preacher's personality, demeanor, reading, or speaking ability? Nor is it a logical fallacy or simply a vicious *argumentum ad hominem* attack.

We have to know and understand what we mean when we critique the sermon and the preacher. To make such a judgmental statement is to show also your own limitations, alongside the shortcomings of another preacher. In your understanding and view of preaching, that assertion may be true, and yet I advise you not to say it to your fellow preachers. Preaching is not a competition, and it is not a song or a dance. It is not a carnival, and it is not a circus show. It is to "build up the church" (1 Cor 14:12).

Think about what saying another person cannot preach actually means. In a certain sense, it can be an indictment of the self, and it distances you from another preacher in a way that is psychologically and spiritually arrogant and just plain ugly. And certainly you do not think of yourself that way. As a teacher, coach, and mentor of preachers, and as a pastor for many years, my calling and my responsibility as a preacher and to preachers is to do the best that I can to constantly prepare myself to become a better teacher and preacher, and to help others who are struggling to prepare and enrich themselves. Preaching and teaching preaching is an awesome act of love for me and can only be done out of love. And yet so many students continue to misinterpret sermon critique as an attack on them—conflating the self with the sermon. Teaching preaching is an awesome and awful responsibility. If you are preaching to people and you do not love people, then you are a joker and a fraud in danger of bringing hellfire and damnation upon yourself.

And if we judge other preachers prematurely, we are setting ourselves up as little judging gods when the truth is that we have no right or authority to judge. Listen up, my beloved, just because you may be popular as a preacher, surrounded by thousands of people on Sunday and folk are telling you that you are a great preacher, stroking your ego with accolades, patting you on the back, and giving you money, satiating your senses, and bowing down at your feet—this does not mean that you are, in fact, a great preacher. There is a qualitative difference between *greatness* and *popularity*, and one does not translate into the other.

Think about it. I know it is hard to face, but you may have crowds and throngs of listeners and parishioners not because you are saying something great, meaningful, and transformative, but it could be that you are saying nothing to challenge folk, nothing to help them take a serious look at transforming their lives, much less transforming the community and world. You might as well be a comedian.

Nobody in the churches that I know is saying to the preacher, "Come over here and transform us." It is more like folk are saying, "We have been making it alright without you before you came to be our pastor." Jesus's preaching and teaching led to death on the cross—not popularity, but unpopularity! Unpopularity is to me more Christological and more theological than popularity. And preachers have no interest in saying that which will lead to social and political revolution—death. In the Gospel of Mark, when Jesus preached, the Pharisees and scribes covered their ears and began immediately plotting to kill him (Mark 2:6-7; Mark 6:1-6). Jesus was unpopular!

If everybody wants to hear us, then maybe, just maybe, it is because what we are saying does not trouble anybody. The sermon makes folk feel good, but it "don't" do them no good, except satiate their egos. The gifted preacher, if you are that, is not always the great preacher, and the so-called great preacher may not be gifted with much truth or holiness at all. Personality, yes. Style, yes. Melodic voice, yes. Charisma, yes. Handsome and "pretty" like Muhammed Ali, yes. Adorned with beauty, yes. But what about love, justice, and truth? What about possessing what St. Augustine, that fourth century North African bishop called the "sweetness of the word" in your everyday life? Jesus says, "But the one who is greatest among you will be your servant" (Matt 23:11). This declaration of Jesus in Matthew's Gospel clashes with our being waited on hand and foot as pastors and bishops seeking to be served rather than or more than anything else. This is a tragedy and travesty.

Listen, I tell you the truth: I've never been considered to be a "great preacher" by the dominant Black church. And not too popular either, even in my own church and community. I have to work hard. I have to study hard, and I have to pray hard just to survive among these entertaining, pop-culture, sound-bite, telegenic, histrionic purveyors of celebrity and popularity. But I tell you what, I may not be popular, and I am surely not great, but the important thing for me is that I do not want to ever be accused of not studying and preparing in a way that advances Black life—or human life, for that matter.

So, it is in the spirit of the ancient rabbis that I seek to be holy by believing that the preacher who reads, re-reads, un-reads, writes, re-writes and studies is participating in a holy act. Studying is an act of holiness and righteousness.[10] The preacher has to develop the whole self—not just prayer and fasting. It is not just the voice, the whoop, the laughter, the cadence, the syncopation, but it is also the mind. The brain, which has a left side and a right side. A cognitive side and an emotional side. Preaching demands the development of the plasticity of the brain in all of its dimensions. All of this helps the preacher to get in front of the text. Get the *self* out of the way first, and then maybe God and the Holy Spirit will allow you to get out in front of the text by sublimating the destructive egotistic self and elevating the word of God, such that the grace of God can open up the text in new and transforming ways.

Getting in Front of the Text

When I left my first pastorate in Norfolk after fourteen years to become the pastor of the Second Baptist Church in Richmond, Virginia, I was not really excited. I was not enthusiastic, not enthralled, and not even sure of why I was uprooting my wife and small children from their hometown and place of birth to go one hundred miles west to Richmond, the former capital of the confederacy. I think about it, I was more sad than anything else, grief-stricken for leaving the church that gave me a start in ministry.

---

10. I am indebted to Professor Peter Ochs, the Edgar Bronfman Professor of Modern Judaic Studies at the University of Virginia, for this concept of studying as a spiritual practice, a holy act.

Richmond and Norfolk in many ways are like night and day. The social climate and the culture are completely different. The Norfolk church was a revolving door. I had nearly five hundred members at the church during my tenure there, and I had over 1,800 people join. Many were in the Marines or Navy, and most were from North and South Carolina, Georgia, and Mississippi—a real cosmopolitan and loving group of folks. And I felt beloved by the people at the church. This is not romanticism. I was very active in the community, advocating for social justice and educational opportunity. On one level, I was quite happy, but on another, I was anxious, feeling that it was time to make a move, to move on to something more challenging. And challenging it was.

When I was called to Second Baptist Church, I was apprehensive and ambivalent. A negative narrative had already begun to be circulated by certain members of the choirs with their diva personalities and purveyors of fiction. The former pastor had died after forty-two years of service. The people had constructed and designed a long process of calling a new pastor. Consultants. Surveys. Background checks. Workshops on all types of leadership stuff. They, like almost all historic Black churches, claimed that they wanted change. They wanted youth development and more participation. They said they wanted the new pastor to be a leader, to transform the existing culture. But this was an exercise in fiction masquerading as truth. Do not misunderstand me here because a lot of people believe they are telling the truth when they are, in fact, lying or deluding themselves.

So, at the end of the process, I was the chosen and selected one—yet I felt like I was on stage, on trial, on display. There was no real joy. I felt like someone was lurking in the shadows with an axe, with a heavy, sharp blade that could come down on my neck at any given moment, or most certainly when I would make a wrong step or say the wrong thing. And it did not take long. Showing up was quite enough!

The first day that I arrived in the office was on a Tuesday morning during the first week of August, the dog days of summer. There were flowers, welcome baskets, and banners symbolizing and signifying joy and celebration, and yet it was a blatant, soon-to-be-revealed negative dialectic. It spoke of how some church folk felt, but not others.

On that first day at the church, I was thirty-seven years old, having been a pastor since I was twenty-three. I began planning for Sunday by meeting and listening to those who represented their various ministries. But they did not use the language of "ministry." There were various "clubs" and "organizations." Language often clarifies or obscures purpose, and words and phrases are important and have to be chosen with precision and care, which is something I had to deal with later. But on that first day, we were working on the church's bulletin for the upcoming Sunday. I asked the church secretary to put a notice in the bulletin about stewardship and tithing, a very basic biblical concept.

"I don't think that you have the *authority* to do that," she responded with alacrity to my request. Before I could say another word, she said, "I have to call somebody first to see if we can allow you to do that."

"Well, blow me down," I said to myself, in the spirit of Huck Finn. This one request made me a threat to the existing status quo. In other words, without hesitation or trepidation, she let me know that the pastoral search committee's desire that the new pastor be a strong leader was empty talk. A fictive narrative. They wanted me to be a follower, not a leader. In the Black church, the pastor becomes the leader after helping folk for many years. Pastoral leadership is not a *de jure* phenomenon.

This new Black church catechism, this baptism in the waters of blatant resistance —waters muddier than the Mississippi River and deeper than the James—caused me to wonder out loud about what kind of purgatory or hell I had gotten myself into. The church secretary's words still ring out as loud as a trumpet and as sharp as a two-edged sword with a serrated blade: "I don't think you, the new pastor, have the authority to do that." These words about pastoral authority made me question not only my experience and sanity, but my calling.

I learned, at that very moment, in that instant, that the call to preach the gospel is indeed a type of foolishness (cf. 1 Cor 1:18). And I was not the pastor, in fact, but the pastor-elect, the de jure pastor. The de facto pastor was the trustee or deacon she had to call to grant permission to do what I asked. The absurdity of her response to my simple request was a sign of things to come. For the record, it takes more than an installation service for the pastor to become the pastor. I emphasize again that it takes helping folk; it takes visiting folk in hospitals, schools, homes, and prisons. It takes helping folk to raise their children and buying them food when there is no meat on the table. It takes sacrifice and a deep abiding love. It takes time! And ultimately it takes helping them with issues of life and death. It takes a generation of funerals and baptisms. It takes a lot of pain and suffering. It takes years of preaching and teaching.

The point I am making is that we really should watch and weigh carefully what we say to folk, how we relate to them with words. The stressors at the church for me were debilitating and almost paralyzing, creating an anxiety that pushed me to the edge of quitting. I was tempted, on more than one occasion, to pack my bags, to gather up my family, my books, and my research papers and go home—to find me a corner to construct a weeping theology of self-pity, a theology of self-doubt, and a theology of cynicism and anger because the distance between the theology and practices of the church and my own understanding and practice of ministry was too great. The chasm was too wide and too fractured by the church's politics of perception and by the institutionalization of tradition and its sacred yet unholy hold on the people of God. There is, in fact, something evil and ugly about our behavior in the church and community. The sense of what I am saying is perhaps expressed best by poetry, rather than prose, particularly by the Langston Hughes poem "Evil Morning" with its haunting lines: "with my feet in the mire / and my heart in a bog."[11]

One autumn evening, just a few months into the job, a large group of people—unruly, boisterous, contentious, and ready to fight—summoned me to a meeting to explain why they disliked me and my leadership style so much and why on certain Sundays I should not even bother to come to church because they were in control of the worship and my very presence was a hindrance to their worship experience and spiritual celebration. My name had been derided in the public square, on city buses and in beauty salons and barber shops, and the church had moved from the carnivalistic to the spectacle as folk were motivated to participate in the drama fueled

---

11. Langston Hughes, "Evil Morning," in *The Collected Works of Langston Hughes* (Columbia: University of Missouri Press, 2001), 2:69.

almost naturally by the gospel music and the discordant sounds of the singers and the preachers.

Under this palpable pressure, I struggled to maintain my sanity and to preach the word of God, but it was more like a burden than a blessing. This was a storm, and even the folk who were in my corner, those who voted to call me to serve as pastor, were having second thoughts and plotting to help form a coup d'état. I was caught in the vortex of a whirlwind, in the center of a brewing storm where there was little to no peace in my soul.

Preaching through a storm is a terrible burden that I do not wish on anyone.[12] I wanted to preach, but I could barely get out of bed, and it was even more difficult to attend the church where I was the pastor in name only. I was sinking into a deep depression—spiritually, physically, and psychologically—and it took every fiber in my mind and body to fight against its destructive forces. I lost my appetite. I lost weight. I lost my hair and almost lost my sanity. Nihilism was trying to take hold of me.

But by the grace of God, I did not lose hope because my faith grew stronger—even soared to new heights. And like in the Gospel of Mark where people were saying that Jesus was a demon, well, they said the same of me and added the addendum that he "can't preach." This narrative is the death of a Black preacher! A type of crucifixion. Unfortunately, in many cases, it is grounded in fiction, or a subjective evil, or dislike of the subject. Now, this dislike is often based on a popular culture ethics that is determined by television, radio, the local church culture, hearsay, rumors, seminarians, and some professors. Even some of my students and interns tend to buy into this most judgmental, subjective, and politically destructive narrative. It is hard for people to think for themselves and to be ethical in their judgments of others. It is a fictive narrative intended to be the death knell of the Black preacher.

This narrative is often advanced by other preachers because behind a pastor's or preacher's problems in the church and the community is usually another preacher or pastor. I say this with a degree of sorrow and shame, but with a conviction that I know to be true. For the people to

---

12.   See, for example, H. Beecher Hicks Jr., *Preaching Through a Storm* (Valley Forge, PA: Judson, 1976).

say that the Black preacher "can't preach" is worse than saying that the doctor or physician cannot heal. It is the antithesis to being what one has laid claim to being. It is an epistemological fallacy. No, it is much more damning than that. It is an attempted ontological negation or castration that applies only to the Black preacher, where the standard is grounded in the performative and the aesthetic. It is an affront to "Being," which is not limited to the self but extends to God.

In other words, for another preacher to say that the Black preacher cannot preach is to say that you question the wisdom of God in calling such a nonperforming person. It is to say that God cannot possibly be God to make a certain preacher so ungifted and Black. It is to say that you are the judge of God's faulty judgments and that God has been mistaken in bestowing on the particular Black preacher, whoever he or she is, the call to preach. It is to completely ignore the anthropological dilemma of the weak and frail preacher, and, in a serious way, it is to drive the nails of crucifixion into Jesus all over again by asserting that God's chosen Black representative of Christ "can't preach." It is to say that the preacher is not a treasure in an earthen vessel, but a trinket in an earthen vessel (cf. 2 Cor 4:7) A treasure? No! A golden coin? No! A pot of silver? No! A wonderful mouthpiece of God? No! A blessing from God to the people of God? No!

To say that the Black preacher cannot preach is to make the preacher an automaton and to make the creative, powerful word of God a fruitless product of material culture, like an assembly line of auto parts. But in spite of the negative, ugly, and even evil words, we have preachers in Black skin get up and "brush their shoulders off," as Jay-Z would say. Then they go back to the study, sit at the desk, and pray that God and the muse will inspire them to work hard to honor that which they have been called to do.

Let us face the truthful reality. Somebody may have heard you on your worse day, when the burdens of life were so heavy upon your heart and soul that you in fact did do a disservice to preaching the gospel. On that day, at that time and place, you or I may have been guilty of not doing what God called us to do: "the preacher couldn't preach." A judgment reserved only for Black preachers and seldom said about the white or non-Black preacher. Preaching is always hard and demands a dedicated and determined desire to do justice to that which you have been called. If you can open your mouth, yes, you can preach. If you can read, re-read, and un-read, yes, you can preach. If you can study and pray, then, yes, you can preach. It may not be with eloquent words of wisdom, as Paul says in 1 Corinthians 2:4. It may not be like Jarena Lee, Dwight Riddick Sr., James Perkins Jr., Charles Booth, Geoffrey V. Guns, Ella Mitchell, Amin Flowers, or Steven Blunt. It may not be like William H. Curtis, William Johnson, Joy Carter Minor, Marcus Allen, or anybody in your family, church, or seminary class, but if God called you to preach, do not let any words by another frail, weak preacher shut you down. Our words to and about one another are often harmful and hurtful. I encourage preachers to learn to build up one another by telling the truth in love and kindness, thereby encouraging one another in the spirit of Christ.

The word of God is more powerful than our words, and the word represents the closing of the sermon. It is the conclusion written in what Thomas G. Long calls "time honored homiletical fashion,"[13] when the preacher wraps up this message with a tribute to the power of God's word. The word of God is alive and active. Its power is not dormant or sedentary, but alive, full of verve and nerve, full of power and strength, full of virtue and victory. The word of God is active and alive, working deep in the heart and mind, and working on our conscience, constructing a new understanding of our relationship with one another and with God.

Love Builds Up, Knowledge Puffs Up

Now about food sacrificed to idols: We know that we all possess knowledge. Knowledge puffs up, but love builds up. The man who thinks he knows something does not yet know, as he ought to know. But the man who loves God is known by God.

—1 Corinthians 8:1-3

More than ten years ago, the United States celebrated the four hundredth anniversary of Jamestown, the first English settlement. But let us not forget that Great Britain was the architect of colonialism and

---

13.   Thomas G. Long, *Hebrews* (Louisville: Westminster John Knox, 1997).

domination of the Other, often the hated Other whose skin was black, brown, or yellow. As African Americans, let us not forget our history and the role that British imperialism played in the colonization of Africa, Asia, the Caribbean. In America, where cotton was king, black slaves picked that cotton for no wages and built Thomas Jefferson's Monticello and the University of Virginia. Let us not forget. Do not let the pomp and circumstance erase our memory of how stony the road has been for Blacks, for Native Americans, and for others who were enslaved by the British Empire.

We have heard a president of the United States and other politicos talk about democracy around the world, a democracy that Black people and poor people still have not fully experienced. Blacks were slaves for over three hundred years in the midst of a democracy, and yet after that we still had to pay poll taxes to vote in the cradle of the democracy. We were lynched and physically and mentally castrated in the land of democracy. American and British democracy has meant domination and subjugation of Blacks and the powerless. Democracy is the language of the majority. It is a principle that by its very nature squashes minorities and quells the voices of dissent. More importantly, it bullies the weak into submission and engulfs the Other into a universalism that obliterates their identity. Democracy has resulted in the systematic erasure of the Other, i.e., Blacks and minorities. Only through un-reading can we develop a more compassionate and more complete understanding of the meaning and practice of democracy.

In 2006, Pope Benedict XVI cited the words of a Byzantine emperor who characterized some of the teachings of the Prophet Muhammad as "evil and inhuman."[14] And yet he says that he did not mean to malign Islam. Knowledge abounds in politics and in religion. Knowledge abounds in Judaism, Christianity, and Islam. The Apostle Paul says, "We know that we all possess knowledge" (1 Cor 8:1b). Yes, we do. It was knowledge of atomic energy and nuclear physics that allowed the United States to hold the distinction of being the only nation in the world to use the nuclear bomb

---

14. Frances D'Emilio, "Vatican Says Pope 'Regrets' Remarks About Islam Founder," *Pittsburgh Post-Gazette*, September 16, 2006, https://www.post-gazette.com/news/world/2006/09/17/Vatican-says-pope-regrets-remarks-about-Islam-founder/stories/200609170251.

against another country, shattering the bodies and buildings of thousands upon thousands of Japanese in both Hiroshima and Nagasaki. The whole world knows this, and that is why they are asking themselves what they should do with their own knowledge of how power is used to perpetuate itself and squash any semblance of rebellion. The knowledge in question is theological. We are worshipping the knowledge instead of praising the Lord.

Knowledge puffs up. Love builds up—it is a relative phenomenon and practice. Paul is not an enemy of knowledge because there is some goodness in knowledge. Knowledge itself is not the enemy, but knowledge, like anything else, can lead to idolatrous behavior. Knowledge devoid of faith and love is a type of idolatrous and dangerous egoism. Knowledge devoid of kindness and compassion is a vile destructive force, capable of emasculating, destroying, and annihilating anything that stands in its path to power and domination. This is the same vaunted knowledge, the same boastful knowledge, and the same vain knowledge that allows our leaders to smirk and smile while talking about American democracy and at the same time dominating the powerless.

"We know that we all possess knowledge," Paul says. He is suggesting that this is not something to boast about. Yes, we all have knowledge—but to boast about our knowledge is no virtue. And by the way, Paul is not complimenting the Corinthian church on their knowledge. This is more an indictment than anything else. Knowledge rightly understood as a gift from God is not something for us to boast about because when we boast about our knowledge as if it were our own, all we are doing is proclaiming our own ignorance. There is an irony here. The more you boast, the more "ignant" (sic) you sound, as my daddy used to say. And we all have to be careful because a little knowledge of self and world is even more dangerous than a lot.

Again, Paul, like so many of us is no enemy of knowledge, God forbid! God's people need all the knowledge we can get, but it is like power. Give people a little authority, and before you know it, it is "done gone to their heads." And you wonder what in the world happened. How did their head swell so big, so fast? Because the more you learn and know, the more you understand your limitations and finitude, and the more you should understand the infinite knowledge, love, and goodness of God.

Yes, my beloved brothers and sisters—do not hate. Do not be mad with somebody who does not seem as capable as you are. We should learn, read, study hard, stay in the library, and burn the midnight oil, but do not forget that it is not knowledge that calms fears and curtails my cravings. It is not knowledge that makes one say "I am sorry" or "Pardon me." I can testify that it is not knowledge that woke me up this morning and enables me to keep on keeping on. No, it is not knowledge. It is not my frail, weak, puffed-up knowledge. It is not knowledge that provides freedom and liberation, because Paul says, "We know that we all possess knowledge." Knowledge puffs up, but love builds up. As a preacher with my little partial knowledge, I want to build up people who have been beaten down, talked about, discouraged, and oppressed.

Again, knowledge puffs up! It swells the ego. Knowledge focuses on the self, creating a negative and false pride. It inflates, makes one haughty and arrogant. It makes one think too highly of oneself. This is head knowledge that has not made an axis through the compassionate heart and through the soul. This knowledge that puffs up is knowledge that has not made the journey through tough life experiences, the journey through trouble and hard times, the journey through sorrow and suffering. This is head knowledge that has not traveled the long winding road of headache or the curvaceous and slippery slope of pain, despair, and dejection. This limited, one-sided knowledge puffs up and makes one walk around like he or she has power over others—indeed, often showing contempt and condescension toward others. This is puffed-up knowledge.

But wait, my beloved preachers of the word. Here is the thesis: love builds up. In Christian ethics and theology, and in Christian practice, knowledge must always lead to love—not puffed-up pride. Love builds up, edifies, builds up character and respect, and creates justice. Love builds up strength in others and the self. Love does good for others. As a matter of fact, love is centered in others, not in the self. It seeks to make others happy. Love builds up the church. Love builds up the community. Love builds up the family, the school, the nation—the world—through the development of behavior, attitude, and disposition.

Love is true knowledge. Love is true understanding. Love is the seat of power. Love is the father of hope and the offspring of godly desire! When you build up those who have been beaten and torn down by the winds of hateful indifference and the torrents of terror that have torn apart hopes and dreams, that is true knowledge. That is love. True knowledge and true love are bound together. They are married to each other with compassion and understanding. When you build up the self-esteem of children and help adults achieve their goals and potential, that is love. When you build up your own character so that you treat the poor with respect and love, so that you give your time to help somebody along the way, that is love. Paul made it even clearer a few chapters later when he wrote: "Love is patient; love is kind; love is not envious or boastful or arrogant or rude. It does not insist on its own way; it is not irritable or resentful" (1 Cor 13:4-5 NRSV).

Preach Good News to the Oppressed

The Spirit of the Lord GOD is upon me, because the LORD has anointed me;
he has sent me to bring good news to the oppressed,
to bind up the brokenhearted, [...] to proclaim the year of the LORD's favor.

—Isaiah 61:1-2 (NRSV)

These words of scripture remind me of the Negro spiritual "Ain't That Good News." I love to watch and listen to the news. This is not a new pastime for me. As a child, I used to walk with my daddy down the back path on the edge of the woods to what we called the Big House, where my grandmother and aunt lived. It was the family's gathering place, and every day around six in the evening, Daddy and I would watch the news. That is how I remember the details of events like the tension-filled Cuban missile crisis and the Bay of Pigs fiasco when the United States tried to overthrow Fidel Castro. I remember the assassinations of the Kennedys, the president and his brother Bobby, and of my hero Martin Luther King Jr., whose face was the symbol of resistance, protest, and poise under pressure. Moreover, King's voice and sharp mind signified Black pride and Black power heretofore unacknowledged in American public discourse. King was a bona fide public intellectual and public theologian. His social activism grew out of his church affiliation and his intellectual acumen.

I remember the invasion of Czechoslovakia by the Soviet Union in the summer of 1968, and I saw images of the thousands upon thousands killed in the Vietnam War. I watched those Black men and women march in the streets of Selma and Birmingham for freedom and justice. I saw the beatings and the dogs attacking old Black women and men, teenagers and children. The television news brought the evils of America's crucible of race and the hatred of Blacks to the eyes of the world, though sanitized by editors and executives. I grew up on the evening news, and now that news is broadcast twenty-four hours a day, I watch CNN, CNBC, FOX, and CBS. I see the oil rigs owned by BP spewing out oil miles from under the Gulf, killing fish and crabs and destroying the Louisiana, Alabama, and Mississippi coast with a thick sludge of oil. And now these same business-people are in charge of American government and politics.

I hear the governors, the senators, and congress talk about trying to reel in Wall Street greed and trying to bring criminal charges against corporations for corruption and for masterminding the housing crisis. But they remain completely unconcerned about public education, public housing, public health, the poor, and the little person. When the democrats and the republicans are concerned about getting reelected, we do hear a few give lip service to helping the poor and the oppressed.

But it is tough being Black and poor. I know firsthand because my family did not have electricity and running water until I was in high school, and we never got much heat in the winter and certainly no air conditioning in the summer. I grew up with outhouses, slop jars, foot tubs, and buckets of water and baths on the weekend only. So, I was glad to get up every morning and go to school, and when the school started serving hot lunches, I was pretty close to heaven. This might explain my love affair with reading, re-reading, and un-reading texts. Life is learning, and learning is life.

The TV and newspapers are filled with news, but it ain't good news. It is bad news: murders, rapes, killings, guns, bullets. Raheem DeVaughn is right in his Marvin Gaye–like rhythm-and-blues ballad "Bulletproof,"[15] where he offers social commentary on the violence in the government and in the community:

> Some will die over oil, kill over land [...]
> We load it, cock it, aim and shoot [...] living like we bulletproof.

Bad news dominates the airways, the internet, and the front pages of the papers, but we know that already. If that were all I had to say to the congregation, I could have stayed at home and pulled the covers over my head in disgust and shame. But that is not why I'm here. I'm here for a different reason, a different motivation, a different spirit. After four hundred years in Egyptian captivity, the prophet Isaiah comes to deliver transforming, earth-shaking, consciousness-shattering good news. The bad news "done come and gone." We have cried long enough, and the pain has been rough and tough, so the prophet comes preaching good news:

> The spirit of the Lord God is upon me, because the LORD has anointed me; he has sent me to bring good news to the oppressed, to bind up the broken-hearted, to proclaim liberty to the captives, and release to the prisoners; to proclaim the year of the LORD's favor. (NRSV)

The kingdom of God in the Isaiah text and in the Negro spiritual song is a "now kingdom" rather than an eschatological one. "I got shoes in that kingdom." The kingdom is as much about this world as it is the next. The demands of the kingdom are such that a confrontation with the powers on the issues of poverty, justice, fairness, and liberation of the oppressed is an urgent enterprise that calls for a new "newness"—an immediacy that cannot be postponed. The immediacy itself is constitutive of liberation, and the preacher is called to the task of bringing about the kingdom of God—now.

Today, social justice as a theory and practice is a holy phenomenon grounded in the word of the Lord. This anointing spirit is foundational to preaching good news to the poor and liberating the oppressed. The language of the prophet in Isaiah 61:1-11 is so integral to the nature and

---

15. "Bulletproof" lyrics by Raheem DeVaughn from his third studio album *The Love and War MasterPeace* (RCA/Jive Records, 2010).

will of God that the writer of the Gospel of Luke places these same prophetic words on the lips of Jesus as a testimony to understanding himself as a preacher and representative of the Sovereign Lord (cf. Luke 4:16-21). The preacher's mission is to announce and bring about social justice and transformation in the church and world. This is what it means for the preacher, the church, and the community to be holy, anointed, and spiritual. The preacher of the word ineluctably is called to understand that our identity as preachers and human beings is related to poor and oppressed peoples all over the world. This means that issues of justice and preaching for transformation are part and parcel of being a minister. This work, this ministry, this calling is essentially about helping the poor, the sick, the lame, the disenfranchised, and the dejected.

Being a prophetic pastor/preacher is about negotiating human affairs such that it demands understanding the depths of the economic, racial, and social issues that Black folk face daily. The preacher is compelled to function in an imperialist and hostile environment. Therefore, it is incumbent upon the preacher to read, interpret, and reread her or his social and political location by creating another, more hopeful, world for oppressed and poor people. In the spirit of Jesus and Martin Luther King Jr., it is important for all to understand that "Rescripting life" is what the Black preacher is called to do every Sunday and every day of the week. This language is another way of saying: "Un-reading the Text."

This is the antithesis of what we hear preachers espousing on radio and television today. They too often are talking about personal prosperity and selfish gain. It is okay to be prosperous if your whole church and community are prosperous, but let us not preach prosperity and live lavishly while the ordinary folk in your church and community are struggling to make ends meet. Let us share the wealth among the people.

The words from the prophet Isaiah, words quoted by Jesus as his first public sermon, redirect the Christian community to the real reason for its existence: "to bring good news to the oppressed; to bind up the brokenhearted; to proclaim liberty to the captives and release to the prisoners; to proclaim or preach the year of the LORD's favor and the day of vengeance of our God; to comfort all who mourn" (Isa 61:1-2 NRSV). These words outline the mission of the preacher/prophet with astounding clarity and simplicity.

In a world that is plagued with dilemma and difficulty, the synagogue, church, and mosque are called to be instruments of God's restoration by bringing good news to the poor and afflicted who have been faithful to God in the midst of trials; healing the hearts of those crushed and dispirited by their experiences; sharing a message of freedom with those bound by poverty, despair, slavery, and other forms of injustice; and proclaiming that the time has come for God to end the season of suffering and bring about God's righteousness and purpose through grace. That is good news. Good news says quite forcefully that you can do it. "You can graduate from high school and college." "You can get a job and no longer be homeless." Good news says that... (Ps 34:11-22).

The Written, Oralized Sermon

The African-American sermon is a speech event, spoken often to a crowd of fifty and then, as Du Bois says, to a thousand.[16] But this phenomenon regarding the verbal process of the preacher is grounded in the psychology and personality of the preacher. This is what I prefer to call *spirituality* or *aesthetics*, which is an integral part of the preaching process. This is what the Apostle Paul termed preaching "with a demonstration of the Spirit and of power" (1 Cor 2:4), and I have talked about this in my book, *The Word Made Plain*, as the act of preaching as interpretation.[17]

The written sermon, when *spoken* by the preacher, often defies the laws of logic and morphs into a spiritual enterprise. It is the *spokenness*, the verbal delivery of the sermon, that harbors the marks of the spiritual and is able to contribute to making the sermon understood and appreciated by the congregation. Elements such as intonation, syncopation, mimicry, gestures (not just of the hands, but the entire body), and the musical delivery or tonality of the sermon that are thought to be ancillary and secondary are, in fact, primary and overlap with the written sermon to help support the sermon as sermon and not just another example of written

16. See W. E. B. Du Bois, *The Souls of Black Folk* (New York: Dover), 1994.

17. See James Henry Harris, *The Word Made Plain* (Minneapolis: Fortress, 2006).

discourse. These are some of the inscribed, external, and spiritual marks of the sermon that are often shunned by white preachers but embraced by Black preachers. Ricoeur also seems to embrace this concept when he states, "In this sense, the inscription in external marks, which first appeared to alienate discourse, marks the actual spirituality of discourse."[18] The written word on the page connects us to something spiritual.

JONAH VI: "The Mystery and the Miracle"

The LORD God appointed a bush, and made it come up over Jonah,
to give shade over his head,
to save him from his discomfort;
so Jonah was very happy about the bush.

—Jonah 4:6 (NRSV)

We will never understand everything about the universe, nor will we understand everything about ourselves and our God, though we would like to. Science and medicine would, no doubt, like to take all the guessing and wonder out of life, but even those equations and calculations cannot explain, cannot even understand, the enormous power and presence of God. Let us face it: we cannot even understand our own dreams, decisions, behaviors, attitudes, anger, and anxiety. We get mad about stuff that we cannot do anything about—stuff that we think we know everything about, and yet we know very little.

I recently saw the most fascinating movie *Dawn of the Planet of the Apes*, which shows how violent and inhuman the white man can be. Even Frantz Fanon's dictum that the Black man yearns to be white and the white man struggles to be human proves to be something of a fallacy because there is no struggle to be human when the goal of life is not freedom and justice, but domination and war. Violence and hate by the apes in the movie were learned from humans, who could not be trusted to bring about peace because humans set themselves apart from apes, whom they call animals. The film shows that the real villains in God's creation are human beings, who do not seem to have much capacity for compassion, love, and peace. In the

18. See Paul Ricoeur, "The Model of the Text: Meaningful Action Considered as Text," *Journal of Social Research* 38, no. 3 (Fall 1971): 535.

film, even Koba, the renegade ape, learned his behavior from being locked in a cage and treated cruelly by humans. And the tragedy is not just that humans treat other species badly, but humans treat each other badly.

Take the movie *Belle*, where the star is a Black girl whose mother is Black and whose father is white. The child is brought to live with her white father's parents in a mansion that even on the screen looks bigger than any mansion I have ever seen. It is the home of the chief justice, a grand manor plantation house sitting back amidst a grove of trees that would make Jonah's gourd vine seem more like a tall weed. Like *Dawn of the Planet of the Apes*, the movie *Belle* is filled with violence at the hand of the white man, where a slave ship filled with African slaves refused to dock at any of the ports because the owners wanted the slave cargo to perish, so they could collect from the insurance company by defrauding the company at the expense of Black lives. And as Mark Twain and Popeye would say, "That ain't the worst." This Black girl's all-white family never allowed her to have dinner with them whenever there were guests because they were ashamed of her being Black. This too is a reflection of the injustice in the hearts and minds of humankind.

The Jonah text says that God "appointed a bush and made it come up over Jonah, to give shade over his head, to save him from his discomfort" (4:6 NRSV). God is the source of our appointments. God can make stuff happen that is inexplicable, that cannot be explained by our limited rationality or our little minds. This bush has what I call a "divine assignment" that is specific and short-term. This is the mystery and the miracle. Keep in mind now that Jonah is sitting on the east side of the city in the heat, the sun, and the wind because he is still mad with God because of God's changing his mind about what Jonah had prophesied to the Ninevites, that in forty days they would be destroyed. Jonah was so mad that he wanted to die. And yet in spite of his madness, in spite of his ugliness, in spite of his sulking, in spite of his whining, God provides him a bush for comfort, a gourd vine to cover his head and protect him from the sun.

God will cover God's people. God is a cover-providing God. God will cover you and save you. God has us covered in spite of our behavior, in spite of our desire to die, in spite of our jealousy, in spite of our anger.

Jonah was all this, and yet God saved him from discomfort. God saves us in spite of ourselves. God saves us because God feels our discomfort, and God's desire is to comfort us. God is our comfort and strength. "Comfort, O comfort my people," says God through the prophet Isaiah (40:1 NRSV). And Jesus says in the Gospel of Matthew, "Blessed are those who mourn, for they shall be comforted" (5:4 NKJV). God provides comfort to Jonah in spite of his attitude and behavior, and "what God does for others, God will do for you," as the Negro spiritual song attests.

Also, there is happiness in the Lord. The love of God seen in the divine covering of a bush that came up one day and was gone the next made Jonah very happy. This is a mystery and a miracle because throughout the whole book, Jonah has never been happy. He has been defiant, but not happy. He has been worried, praying that God would not forget him, saying while among the entrails of the fish, "As my life was ebbing away, I remembered the LORD; and my prayer came to you, into your holy temple" (2:7). But Jonah has not been happy.

Jonah has also been obedient, the second time around. He preached what God told him to say to the Ninevites. But we have no indication that he was happy about it. And now in the text, this is the first sign, the first time Jonah is happy: "Jonah was very happy about the bush" (4:6). This is the *mysterium*, the mystery of God. This is a miracle that God can do. God can turn our frowns, our furrowed brow into a smile. God can turn our complaints into praise. God can turn our defiance into delivering God's word. God can change God's mind, and God can change your mind. God can put shade over your burning head and cover you from the heat, whether it is an east wind, a scorching sun, a sickness, a disappointment, a bad relationship, a confused and wayward spirit, a wandering mind, a lonely heart, or a mad, bad, sad attitude because God can make us smile as the Lord enables us to see another day.

FIRST WRITING/ PREACHING

Talking Back to the Devil

The written word is weak.

—Annie Dillard, *The Writing Life*

JONAH VII: "A Bigger Concern"

But when dawn came up the next day, God appointed a worm
that attacked the bush, so that it withered.
When the sun rose, God prepared a sultry east wind,
and the sun beat down on the head of Jonah
so that he was faint and asked that he might die.
He said, "It is better for me to die than to live." But God said to Jonah,
"Is it right for you to be angry about the bush?"
And he said, "Yes, angry enough to die."
Then the LORD said, "You are concerned about the bush,
for which you did not labor and which you did not grow;
it came into being in a night and perished in a night.
And should I not be concerned about Nineveh, that great city,
in which there are more than a hundred and twenty thousand persons
who do not know their right hand from their left, and also many animals?"

—Jonah 4:7-11 (NRSV)

Many of us major in the minor things of life. Our world view and our imagination are so small and so localized that we appear to have lived our lives on a dead-end street with a brick wall at the end of it, so that we are hemmed in by our neighbors and the few houses on Mango Street, or the Avenue, or the Boulevard. Yes, we spend our time preoccupied with what is happening in the house next door. We are like Mrs. Kravitz on the old television show Bewitched. She was always worrying her husband, Abner, about the strange things that the neighbors Tabitha, Darrin, or Samantha were doing. We are not much better.

Our concerns are so narrow, so small, so parochial, so internal, and so grounded in our own ego and self-serving interests. We are a "my" generation—a generation of big needs and wants, but a generation of little ideas and little concerns. We are clones of Jonah. We suffer from a pathological case of Jonah-isms, which is a plethora of fickle behavior, illogical actions, and an anger that is misplaced, misdirected, and misguided. Listen, we have seen this behavior; we have played this scene. This is *deja vu*. How many times do we have to hear Jonah rant and rave, pine and whine, weep and cry about wanting to die? He needs to get his anger under control or be angry about the right thing—not about the grace and goodness of God that is extended to all, sinners and renegades alike.

This particular text teaches us that we cannot spend our time and energy concerned about the little stuff. We spend so much time—too much time—being concerned about things that we cannot do anything about. God says to Jonah, "You are concerned about the bush, for which you did not labor and which you did not grow; it came into being in a night and perished in a night." Yes, this is a good thing that Jonah is concerned about the bush. It shows God getting Jonah to understand God's vantage point. In the same way, Jonah has concern for the bush, God also has concern for the people of Nineveh.

Talking Back to the Devil: Preaching Jesus Christ

Jesus, full of the Holy Spirit, returned from the Jordan
and was led by the Spirit in the wilderness,
where for forty days he was tempted by the devil.
He ate nothing at all during those days, and when they were over,
he was famished.

—Luke 4:1-2 (NRSV)

This is a battle of wits and will. An epic battle between the forces of good and the forces of evil. This is a battle between Jesus and the devil, between Satan and the son of God. Jesus is saying in effect, "Get behind me, Satan" as he said to Peter on the road to Jerusalem (Matt 16:23). Luke calls the tempter "the devil" in this very dramatic episode of scripture. This is a battle between two kingdoms—between God and the powers of evil. The devil has real power and authority over those who submit themselves to his rule.

I worry a lot about all people, but Black people in particular. It is a natural way of life for me to worry about my sons. We worry about our children—about their safety, their well-being. We worry that somebody will take advantage of their kindness, their naiveté, their inexperience, their eagerness to trust folk and to belong. We often worry about those whom we love: our families, friends, churches, and communities.

The devil knows that Jesus is physically hungry. After being in the wilderness for forty days, the devil tries to tempt him to satisfy his human bodily hunger. The devil says, "If you are the Son of God, command this stone to become a loaf of bread." Jesus answered him, "It is written, 'One does not live by bread alone'" (4:3-4). Jesus disciplines his desire in his response. Yes, human beings have needs and wants. Some are physical—sexual and appetitive. These desires are associated with the physical body, the satisfaction of the body, the flesh, which is weak, weary, and worn. In this case, the devil offers a stone, but this stone is a metaphor for anything that satisfies human bodily desire at its weakest point of need. We need

107

food, sex, and water. We need to pleasure the body. We need bread to satisfy our hunger. This is not allegorical.

This is, however, metaphorical, and it is also metonymical. Yes, bread symbolizes something real and satiating. Think of the wilderness as a place where you have no access to the things you are used to. This is like forty days of no smoking or no drinking alcohol. Forty days of being in a smoke-free zone. Forty days in the wilderness. Forty days of being booze free. No beer. Forty days. No cigarettes. Forty days of no swigging and no swilling. Forty days of no "rolling in the deep" and forty days of "no satisfaction." Move over, Adele, Mick Jagger, and Otis Redding.

The devil suggests that if you have the power to exempt yourself from certain struggles and sufferings, then you should do whatever it takes. If you have the power, the money, the swagger, the rap, the game, the edge, the talk, or the persuasive power to satisfy your urges, your needs, your wants, or your desires, then turn the stone into bread. You just got paid. Go to the club, if you are capable. If you have the power, then turn the stone into bread to satisfy your hunger, to satiate your desire. Light the cigar to calm your quaver.

Some of us are, indeed, "bread alone" folk. Feel good for today folk. Satisfy my desire right now folk. Damn the future, live for today folk. But bread alone is not enough! You have got to talk back to the devil, because the devil is smart and clever. Cunning. Capitalizing on your very vulnerable, convenient occasions to doubt your own strength. Jesus answered the devil by quoting from the Torah, saying, "One does not live by bread alone" (Deut 8:3 NRSV).

> Then the devil led him up and showed him in an instant all the kingdoms of the world. And, the devil said to him, "To you I will give their glory and all their authority; for it has been given over to me, and I give it to anyone I please. If you, then, will worship me, it will all be yours." Jesus answered, "It is written, 'Worship the Lord your God, and serve only him.'" (Luke 4:5-8 NRSV)

We are called to worship God. And worship God alone. We are called to serve no other deity, no other power, no other god. To do so is idolatry. It does not matter what that other object or power is. Jesus rejects this promise of possessions and political power of all the kingdoms of the world. Glory and authority—that is what we as preachers often crave. We do not have many preachers like Jesus because preachers seem to love kingdoms and power. Big churches and bishop status. Kingdoms of this world.

In his answer, Jesus uses the words found in Deuteronomy 6:12-14, when Moses warned Israel not to follow other gods and not forget the Lord. Again, quoting from the Torah, Jesus says worship is for God and God alone. Not the pastor or the bishop. Not the choir. Not the church. Not the building. Not possessions of houses and land. Not our achievements or what little money and power we have. No! Worship God alone. Our theology and philosophy should be to tell the devil, "You can't give me *nothing*. You can't promise me *nothing*. You can't pay me enough. You can't persuade me enough. No person, no politic can lure me away from God. Worship belongs to God alone, and God only shall we serve." Talk back to the devil like Jesus did and say to all the devil's promises of glamour and glitter that it is written that we should worship the Lord our God, and him only we serve.

This devil does not give up, and because of that fact, the text teaches that we have to be on our Ps and Qs in dealing with the devil. The devil is shrewd. The devil can quote scripture too, so everybody quoting scripture "ain't" saved, neither holy nor sanctified. In the first two parts of this temptation, the devil constructs a narrative saying to Jesus that if you are the son of God, then do this. And each time Jesus quotes scripture to counter the devil's tempting proposals. Now, the devil steps up his own game with the ultimate trickery by quoting scripture to Jesus.

In Psalm 91:11-12, the scripture promises "for [God] will command his angels concerning you to guard you in all your ways. On their hands they will bear you up, so that you will not dash your foot against a stone" (NRSV). In his twisted interpretation, the devil says that the scripture means that angels will bear (hold) Jesus up if he jumps from a height like the pinnacle of the Jerusalem temple. But Jesus answers him, "It is said, 'Do not put the Lord your God to the test'" (Luke 4:12 NRSV). Jesus knows that he has no right to manipulate God and neither do we. Do not test God. Trust God, but do not test God for your personal purposes.

Now, for many preachers today who love the spectacular and the limelight of the television cameras, this would have been the perfect opportunity to claim a literal "jump by faith" and a "made-for-television moment." Clearly, this challenge by the devil would have been welcomed as a sign of being "blessed and highly favored" by those who seek glamor, glory, and perceived moments to promote themselves over others.

After tempting Jesus with kingdoms, bread, and the promise that the angels should catch him if he jumped from the pinnacle of the Jerusalem temple, the devil then retreated, but not for long. "When the devil had finished every test, he departed from him until an opportune time" (4:13 NRSV). The devil is busy, my friends. Every day, every hour there is a battle for our children and our youth, and adults are not exempt from the tempter's snare.

JONAH VIII: "When God Answers Prayer"

Then Jonah prayed to the LORD his God from the belly of the fish, saying,
"I called to the LORD out of my distress, and he answered me;
out of the belly of Sheol I cried, and you heard my voice."

—Jonah 2:1-2 (NRSV)

There is no situation too dire, too phenomenal, too hopeless, or too grand that we cannot pray for deliverance. Because of our own frailties and our tendency to bestow our limitations on God, I know we sometimes think that God is a reflection of us, rather than acknowledging that God is self-sufficient. God is not lacking in any attribute, which means that God does not need us—but we are in a real and terrible need of God. Let us take for example the turmoil in the world today: in St. Louis, Missouri, right here in the United States. Am I dreaming? Is this deja vu? Have not we been in this movie, this theater before? Black boys and men are now being hunted down and killed by the new Bull Connors of our cities throughout the South and in middle America, where the same

Mississippi River of Mark Twain's novel *Huckleberry Finn* is still a symbol, the dialectic of slavery and freedom. A dialectic of epic proportions.

I tell young Black males here in America not to give the police any reason to murder you like a hog or hunt you down and kill you and then hide behind the Blue wall of law enforcement, when Black folk have had enough injustice experiences with hate-filled police. The police in America have *never* been on the side of Black people—much less protected them— and my advice today is that we need to think and pray hard before ever calling them because they know mainly how to kill Black people and get away with it. Not long ago it was killing a Black man in New York, then killing of a Black teenager outside of St. Louis. Black people cannot even walk down the street without being mugged by another Black or shot by the police. This is the embodiment of the *metaxological*, the betweenness of life and death evident every day a Black person wakes up. Black people today, like the slaves, can know law only as an enemy!

It seems like civil rights and all the things that Martin Luther King Jr., Rosa Parks, and Fannie Lou Hamer fought for continue to escape most Black people. Other marginalized groups have benefited more from the struggle for civil and human rights, and from laws that forced the nation to be more humane toward one another. More civil, more humane toward everybody except the Black male, who is still being gunned down by the police and often by his own brothers and sisters. Many thousands of Blacks marched, protested, and died for the right to be treated human, and that dream still has not been fulfilled.

There was a time in the early nineties that one could barely walk down Idlewood Avenue and Meadow Street in Richmond, Virginia, without being threatened, mugged, shot, or killed. But today, when areas in the Randolph community such as Idlewood Avenue and Meadow Street have become inhabited by whites, it is suddenly a safe place to walk. I see people—white people, Asians, and Indians—any time of night on the streets of Randolph and near the West End because it is now miraculously safe. It is the same thing in other areas such as Church Hill and the Carver area and throughout the city. But let us face it: it is still not safe for Blacks—Black males, in particular. So, it is always prayer time for our people who know something about prayer, like Jonah.

Jonah is Black! He is constantly struggling with God. He is struggling with himself. He has been in the depths of the sea, the depths of Sheol, the underworld. *Sheol* means a place for the dead, a place of darkness; it is hell. Black people know something about hell, and we have not had to go to the bottom of the Mediterranean Sea to experience it. From crossing the Atlantic Ocean to the shores of the American South, Blacks have been to hell. Jonah was running from the Lord and got caught on a stormy sea. Black men are just walking down the street and being forced to run from the police or the Neighborhood Watch in a vain effort to survive because they are often killed anyway.

In the text, Jonah goes from one belly to another: the belly of the fish, the belly of the sea—in the belly of Sheol—in the depths of hell to being in the belly of the fish. There is a difference in being in the belly of the sea and being enclosed in the belly of the fish. Jonah remembers that he was once in the belly of hell and now he is in the belly of the fish.

He has moved from grief to gratitude. He is glad to be in the belly of the fish. Jonah knows the difference between being in the depths of hell and being in the fish. He prays and God answers his prayer.

A New Method of Homiletic Interpretation JONAH IX: "When God Repents"

When God saw what they did, how they turned from their evil ways, God changed his mind about the calamity that he had said he would bring upon them; and he did not do it.

—Jonah 3:10 (NRSV)

During any warm, sunny day, the story of Jonah should conjure up images of being on the beach somewhere—Virginia Beach, Miami Beach, Meliá Nassau Beach, or the beaches in Jamaica, St. Thomas, or St. Martin. After he has been vomited up by the big fish (often characterized as a whale), Jonah finds himself on a Mediterranean beach. He has been disobedient and downright stubborn in his response to God's directive, and now he finds himself praying and doing what God had asked him to do in the first place. The only thing God wanted him to do—the only thing God asked him to do—was to go to Nineveh, that wicked city, and "proclaim or preach" the message God gave him. Yet, he refused to do what God asked, and he ended up in "hell and beyond." After all of this, he now decides that he better do what God tells him to do.

So, as I read this text, I see where Jonah repents. He turns from his wrongheaded actions. He changes directions, like so many of us need to do today. If you are like Jonah, determined to do what you want to do in spite of what God has directed you to do, and if you are so caught up in yourself and determined that your way is better than God's way, then sometimes God has a way of showing us that God is God and we are not. God allows us to do our own thing, exercise our own judgment, determine our own direction, and go the wrong way and do the wrong thing long enough for us to come to our senses, like the younger brother in the parable of the prodigal son (cf. Luke 15:11-32).

Some of us have been out there doing everything we are big enough to do when we got in deep trouble—gambling away the mortgage money; refusing to pay child support; drinking every Friday, Saturday, and Sunday; swigging yourself into a drunken stupor; dancing the night away from one club and beer fest to another. Our deep trouble was just like being in the belly of the big fish, the whale, at the bottom of the sea. We too are drowning in Sheol—in one hell or another, unable to get a grip on our lives. We all suffer from what I call the "Jonah syndrome," which means that we do not listen to God until we have done what we want to do and said what we want to say and gone where we want to go—as far away as we can get from where God told us to go. Nineveh is one place and Joppa is a long distance from Nineveh.

Our actions are seen and heard by God, and our actions affect God. God repents when we repent of our evil ways. God is pleased. God feels our contrition and changes God's mind about us as we turn away from evil. These Ninevites are evil. Unfortunately, some of these Baptists, Presbyterians, Episcopalians, Methodists, et al. are evil. These relatives are evil. These Richmonders, Baltimoreans, and Bostonians are evil. These evangelicals, missionaries, choir members, and ushers all have evil ways. These human beings are the same in weakness and egoism. We are all Ninevites! But when the prophet Jonah spoke what the Lord prompted him to say—"Forty days more, and Nineveh shall be overthrown!" (3:4 NRSV)—the people changed their ways. They repented, and our scripture text says, "When God saw what they did, how they turned from their evil ways" then God repented, changed his mind (3:10).

This is great. God is a God who can adapt God's punishment or bestow God's grace, and we are a people who can change our ways. Look at the great possibilities that reside in us as a people, as a city, as a church community, as a family. Listen up, my beloved brothers and sisters: People can change and people do change. In the book of Jonah, it is abrupt and sudden. Cataclysmic and transformative. When the Ninevites hear the message of destruction and realize they have forty days to turn their lives around—their hearts, minds, and actions—they repent. They had been acting evil a long time! They had been sinning a long time! They had been ugly and violent a long time! But they heard God's message and repented.

I do not care how long you have been acting evil. I do not care how long you have been doing the wrong thing, living wrong, talking wrong, or running the streets, chasing after hedonistic pleasures rather than pursuing justice and righteousness. God promised punishment and pain—but when we change our evil ways, when we turn from the ways of the world, when we repent, when we change directions and realize that God's judgment is no joke—then God is powerful enough. God is gracious enough. God is big enough. God is generous enough. God is compassionate enough. God is loving enough to repent of what God said God would do and not do it. In this text, God's actions seem to depend on our actions. God holds no grudges like we do! God makes no declarations and promises that God cannot keep, but God is glad *not* to keep some of his promises if it means that God's people can hear and heed God's word.

RE-WRITING/PREACHING

A New Method of Interpretation

> *In the coming world*
> *New prizes are*
> *To be given.*
>
> —Don L. Lee, *We Walk the Way of the New World*

Preaching and Narrative

It is my belief that one's personal narrative, though surrounded by a whole host of witnesses, is yet encumbered by a fictive that escapes the consciousness of us all. In other words, we not only lie to others, but we lie first to ourselves. This is the art of self-deception. Nevertheless, our personal story inhabits and inhibits our experiences and our telling, retelling, and writing about things as varied as politics and the ethics and theology of reading and writing. Even the telling of our personal stories, that is, the story of our lives, is an exercise in narrative hermeneutics and the meaning of revelation.

In telling our stories, we are engaging in an ethical discussion of the self and the writing of fiction about the self. For example, when I ask my students during the first few days of class to describe themselves in one or two words, they deliberately and intentionally avoid a significant portion of truth. The truth is that this may in fact be unintentional because of the lack of consciousness regarding the self. They present only one side of a dialectical or multidimensional self, and that side is described in ideal, positive words or language and phrases such as "I am a loving, kind, and compassionate person" or "I am strong, forgiving, and peaceful." Always positive! Always fictive!

And when I say to them that *fictivity* is the order of the day in their self-description and that they are pretty good novelists or fiction writers when it comes to the self, they not only seem amazed, but they even get angry at me for advancing such an interpretation or analysis of their self-description. The truth is that I am simply trying to get them to understand that the words and language they use are critical to their theology and that their narrative is a type of ethical discourse that should be grounded in a more complex, clear, and truthful understanding of the self, however undiscovered that self tends to be.[1] More importantly, our narratives and personal stories in the language of Adam Zachary Newton "implies simply narrative as ethics: the ethical consequences of narrating story and fictionalizing person, and the reciprocal claims binding teller, listener, witness, and reader in that process."[2] No one is any better than James Baldwin and Zora Neale Hurston.

Our stories, those about ourselves and others, are generally making an ethical claim in spite of our thinking and believing that we are telling the truth, especially about ourselves. Sometimes our words and language are a far cry from the truth, as evidenced by the interpretation of the Other. We always interpret the Other through a different lens, a more glazed lens, than we interpret the self. So, when it comes to the self, memory and truth vis-à-vis honesty and fairness have a slippery hold on our consciousness.

I infuse this chapter with a brief narrative about my own life of reading and then vector toward my discussion of re-reading and un-reading, before finally relating both of these concepts to writing—particularly Jesus's writing on the ground, as he does in John 8:1-11. I also claim that Jesus's saying "You have heard that it was said [...] but I say to you..." (cf.

---

1. See Carl Jung, *The Undiscovered Self* (New York: Signet, 2006).

2. Adam Zachary Newton, *Narrative Ethics* (Cambridge, MA: Harvard University Press, 1995), 11.

Matt 5:27-28) is a manifestation and demonstration of his reading and un-reading of scriptural texts.

My claim here is that there is an intricate correlation between my own personal story and the hermeneutics of reading and un-reading and that one's relationship to his or her own story either enables or prohibits one's ability to understand and explain the scriptural text. As one becomes more adept in interpreting her or his own life experiences through expanding one's horizons, thus enabling a greater awareness, then the preacher can begin to understand other texts such as scripture, congregation, and community.

But all of this starts with the self and with the recognition that self-understanding is a lifelong process and project. "Know thyself," says Socrates, with the understanding that such knowledge is almost impossible to obtain, let alone to understand and practice. The story of the self—the narrative self—is the beginning of hermeneutics because we are so distanced from our own consciousness of self, that is, our own self-understanding. The Black poet Don L. Lee tells the reader to "start with the itch and there will be no scratch. Study yourself."[3] This is a type of phenomenology of the self that I claim is critical for the preacher as she or he begins to try to untangle, unravel, and untie texts in pursuit of transformative and liberating sermonic discourse. All of this precedes method and traditional exegesis. And yet it is a part of both method and interpretation. Every preacher needs a method of sermon preparation that helps to give the sermon structure and clarity—coherence. Without a clear method of sermon construction, the preacher is subject to be haphazard and ill equipped to write and deliver the sermon. The powerful transformative sermon is grounded in homiletical method and theological/philosophical rigor.

Self-Narrative Hermeneutics

I was born without a clear consciousness of what poverty meant. This is a sociocultural moment in my own history. I was rich in spirit and

---

3. See Don L. Lee, *We Walk the Way of the New World* (Detroit: Broadside, 1970), 65.

blessed with good health; however, I had to go to school to understand that we were economically poorer than the children I sat beside in the classroom. This was evidenced by material lack. From the school bus window, I saw the houses pass by; some few were as raggedy as ours, but others were split-levels or old-style farmhouses, and a few were California-style postmodern brick houses with carports and attached garages. In stark contrast, we lived in a two-room shanty built and expanded to four rooms by my father's and mother's own hands. We were without indoor plumbing and without electricity until 1968, when I was in the tenth grade. There were ten of us, in terms of birth order, and I was what William Desmond termed the *metaxological*, the middle of the clan, the fifth child caught between the beginning and the end.

I could always unveil or unravel some semblance of truth in search of authenticity and clarity of life's purpose. I have not been totally or absolutely able to live up to this self-imposed high and lofty ideal. But my gift in search of this pragmatic ideal can be attributed in large part to reading. At least this is my story, my narrative ethic. If my sense and memory are correct, I was "born reading," in the sense that no one ever formally taught me how to read a word or a sentence. Like a singer with musical notes, I could string letters together into words and words into sentences without any knowledge of the linguistic terms coined by Ferdinand de Saussure like *langue* and *parole*.

Semantics and rhetorical flair have been my gift. After being bullied and threatened for speaking, reading, and writing throughout high school, I graduated at seventeen and went to work as a laborer in a cigarette factory for the summer and then onto college in the fall. After graduating from college in three and a half years, I enrolled and came to the graduate school of theology at Virginia Union University. I have been associated with the school in one way or another ever since. I have been on the fringes, trying to balance the real, gritty, hard work of the church and community with the quasi-luxury of teaching young and old graduates and undergraduates in the areas of preaching, literature, practical theology, philosophical theology, and philosophy. My personal project has been creating and forging a nexus between theory and practice, that is, between church administration and worship and between the church and the academy—with both students and church members kicking and screaming in an effort to maintain the status quo, whatever their perception of that is.

I was first called to pastor a very nourishing and supportive church in Norfolk, Virginia, where I was given the opportunity to learn and to become a community social justice activist, advocating for Black and poor people and dabbling with politics. I lost a bid for election to the Norfolk City Council, but I won the hearts of a lot of poor and disenfranchised Blacks who lived in housing projects and on the other side of the city or the underside of culture. In the church, I fought to get one of the first women in the city licensed to preach at a time when it was very unpopular and often dangerous to the success of your ministry, not to mention dangerous to your physical body and mental stability.

I have taught in all areas of practical theology, which has made me determined to rethink the "philosophical" as the "practical" and the practical as the philosophical, infusing homiletics with the social sciences and humanities. I have sought to turn the practical on its head and figure out how I could bridge the *aporias*, or the gaps, between what was historically bifurcated and still remains so in the traditional nomenclature of theological education.

I struggle to be a *practical intellectual*, that is, a *reflective practitioner*. A scholar and an intellectual are not necessarily the same because an intellectual may or may not have a college or graduate degree and a scholar with masters and doctoral degrees may not be much of an intellectual. The only reason for this specific reference is to say that the preacher may serve the church and the public square well if she or he seeks to develop the self in relationship to the Other in such a way as to foster a nexus between this unnecessary but very real dialectic. My students are asked to do a lot of reading for the sake of expanding their interest in reading, which will lead to learning how to un-read texts so that their sermons can be prophetic and transformative, re-describing the world and creating a new world for the poor and oppressed.

The struggle of the preacher is also to learn how to love those persons in the church and community as much as she or he loves the self.

The preacher who is driven by something other than agape love—whether fame, popularity, notoriety, or acceptance—will be easily and prematurely disappointed. This tangled ontology of the preaching self is grounded in a "dialectic of being" that is forever being shaped by the culture (*bildung*) and the context of life, not to mention the ego. The Apostle Paul writes that "love does not seek its own" (1 Cor 13:5 NKJV). I say this because it seems that too many preachers and seminary faculty members develop a distaste, a dislike, and even a disdain for the people of the church, except when the people are elevating them to new heights by their words or deeds. This is something that we all need to guard against. This is the essence of material culture, expressed in its most vulgar and capitalistic form. A type of pimping the Black Church.

In this sense, and I do not mean to be too hortatory or axiological here, preaching cannot and should not be about material prosperity as an ultimate goal or the *telos* of ministry. Instead, the sermon is a type of mimesis but not of another preacher; it is a creative act of representing, reconstructing, restating, re-reading, and un-reading the word of God all over again—Sunday after Sunday. It is in its creative dimensionality, its social imagination, that it has the power to transform some marginal element of existence into something else—something new and different, or at least a different direction of thought. A different direction of action, creating a new world.

This creative dimension of the sermon enables me to say to you that every day I pray that God will speak anew to my situatedness, my context, my very existence and being. In hearing this divine creative voice of God, my ability to create a new sermon becomes more and more grounded in God's creative power and less and less in the weak, fickle, frail self, which is always struggling to get its bearing in the world. The preacher is always trying to reach uncharted rhetorical and linguistic shores in an effort to forge a brand new world—a world of love, justice, and peace.

The preacher is called to be a lover and scholar of scripture interpretation, focused on deciphering meaning for the oppressor and the oppressed from scripture. Scripture interpretation is a theological, philosophical, sociological, political, and pragmatic praxis grounded in the context and consciousness of the preacher, reader, and hearer more so than in the author of the text. There is an inherent weakness in every spoken or written word, as the writer Annie Dillard says,[4] including the writings in the biblical text. Language is vulnerable in the same way we are. In other words, a text is not simply a line of words releasing a single "theological" meaning, but a text is a "multi-dimensional space in which a variety of writing, *none of them original,* blend and clash. The text is a tissue of quotations drawn from the innumerable centres of culture."[5] But the text is also tissue in a generative way. Barthes makes this clear when he writes, "Text means tissue; but hitherto we have always taken this tissue as a product, a ready-made veil, behind which lies, more or less hidden, meaning (truth), we are now emphasizing in the tissue, the generative idea that the text is made is worked out in a perpetual interweaving; lost in this tissue—this texture— the subject unmakes himself, like a spider dissolving in the constructive secretions of its web."[6]

It is, therefore, the preacher's responsibility to strengthen the weak and wilting written and spoken word or text. This strengthening can occur first through reading and then un-reading the text as a homiletic practice in the journey and struggle toward understanding and explanation through the sermon. If French literary theorist Roland Barthes is correct in saying that the text is "a tissue of quotations," then clearly it is unoriginal to the core and, more than that, we do not know who the authors of these blended and clashing quotations are! But we do not need to know because knowing this information does little to help us get in front of the text through reading and un-reading the text.

To explain the text is to understand that it has to be read and re-read in order to be un-read of the language and presumed intention of the author, who potentially is as oppressive and maybe even racist as a host of Christian believers have demonstrated since the beginning of the Common Era. This means that un-reading the text is not simply an act of

---

4. Annie Dillard, *The Writing Life* (New York: Harper Perennial, 2013).

5. Roland Barthes, *Image-Music-Text* (New York: Hill and Wang, 1977), 146, emphasis added.

6. Barthes, *The Pleasure of the Text* (New York: Hill and Wang, 1973), 64.

reading, but it is an advanced defiant act of reading and re-reading until the un-reading of the text becomes clear; therefore, the clarity of the text is unmasked and unfolded via this process. So, echoing some of the historical Black preachers, it is in this sense that Paul Ricoeur is right when he asserts that meaning is a social and cultural expression addressing the needs of the hearers.

Un-reading the text is the ultimate powerful practice of interpretation as reinterpretation, insofar as it addresses the needs of Black people in particular and oppressed people in general. More particularly, since the text, without being un-read, is so often hegemonic, it can only begin to address the "real down-home" issues of Black life through the process of un-reading. Cultural social expression and individuality is the act of asserting Black identity without apology and without fear of retribution.

Meaning is not an isolated phenomenon divorced from the community and the struggles of its people. Meaning is then contextual, such that textual meaning or interpretation seeks to make sense of the senseless acts of evil that cause people to both pray and cuss, to weep and cry in the absence of joy and in the thick of sorrow and pain. This dialectic ontology is the nature of being Black, in spite of whatever else may characterize one's personality.

> To explain the text then means primarily to consider it as the expression of certain socio-cultural needs and as a response to certain perplexities well localized in space and time.[7]

And what could be more perplexing than the lack of consciousness surrounding the historical and current suffering and pain of Black people—some self-inflicted and others inflicted by the architects and sustainers of the status quo from slavery to the present. That status quo has historically meant the violation of Black humanity, supported and practiced by traditional European liberal theology and ethics. And the white church—both Protestant and Catholic—in its practice of racism and religion reflects a gross piety and indifference that is devoid of social consciousness and

---

7. Paul Ricoeur, *Interpretation Theory* (Fort Worth: Texas Christian University Press, 1976), 90.

commitment to justice and love (devoid of Christ) regarding confronting racism, injustice, hatred, and evil in church and society.

As I have said, Black suffering seems to be outside the consciousness of most whites and even some Blacks during this age of instant media exposure, where the "white policeman," as metaphor and *metonomy* for law and order, is unconcerned that he is being recorded and streamed live on Facebook and Twitter while he murders another young Black male with the camera rolling and the baby in the back seat screaming. Or for the Black man who was walking away with his hands up, as in the case of Terence Crutcher in Tulsa, and the police said, "He was reaching for something." Not a gun. Not a weapon. But more like reaching for heaven or reaching for the stars. This is the meaning of trauma. Social media be damned. The law has indeed been the enemy of Black people from slavery to the present.

The expression and response to the needs of Black people is clearly what is called for in sermons, books, movies, classrooms, and conversations in the local church, universities, and broader community. I do not have a universal explanation of any scriptural text because the text is not universal. It is particular, and it is contextual, and it is local. It is also *unoriginal*, and it is intertextual. Again, that is why your sermon must be your own and not constructed by someone else—not by commentary, another preacher, the internet, or sermons.com. And the forces that engulf me are likewise localized in space and time. This is why the local church harbors the ways and means for making a difference, for helping to transform our wilderness spaces into places of habitation rather than uninhabitable and inhospitable jungles, war zones, and comfort zones that breed complacency and disinterest.

To explain a text is to be able to *unsay the said* and conversely to say the unsaid. Likewise, to explain a text is to read the un-read, and to un-read the already read. Un-reading the text is the highest form of reading. I repeat, un-reading is the penultimate form of reading. This is the essence of freedom and liberation because I am no longer bound by anything I have read or anything I have said, for that matter. I am free. Praise the Lord, I'm free! I am free to un-read the already-read text.

My homiletics lectures tend to include a type of "showing," a demonstration, because I often seek to meld and merge weak written discourse with spoken language. This is what the preacher does: he or she writes the sermon and then speaks the sermon off the page and into the hearts and minds of the listeners. The coming together of the written and the spoken sermon harbors more power than just the written or just the spoken sermon. This may fly in the face of conventional wisdom, but I think that the spoken sermon is the second part of the development of the sermon, with the first part being the written discourse. The writing of the sermon requires a certain precision and discipline that often escapes the spoken sermon when it is not written as a prelude to being spoken.

This is not meant to be limiting and restraining, but rather it is intended to be the ultimate expression of freedom, a combination and merger of the written and the spoken. The writing of the sermon as the second stage of the preaching process puts the preacher "dead in the middle" of the semantics of the text and the depth or "deeper" semantics of the sermon. The sermon must be the prophetic word that re-creates and re-describes the world. It is sermonic discourse grounded in textuality that transforms this old world into something new—a brand new world.

Un-reading is an act of hermeneutic suspicion and homiletic subversion. It is an act of enormous imagination and creativity, which the sermon is compelled to reflect—not the same old interpretations handed to us by the Enlightenment and by modernity and post-modernity. As Thomas Hobbes, René Descartes, Thomas Locke, and Immanuel Kant represent this stronghold on western philosophy, I claim that any philosophy that fails to mention American chattel slavery as the antithesis to the Enlightenment is in fact *unenlightened* and ungodly, a deliberate and systematic avoidance of the texts or Torah and Gospel that speak of justice and righteousness and God's loving kindness. Let us not allow our preaching to become idolatrous and thin as tissue paper, a thinness seen in some biblical texts and often running rampant in sermonic discourse engulfing the Black and white church on the regular. The white church seems to have little to no interest in correlating the gospel message with issues of race and justice. Martin Luther King Jr., in his now classic and prophetic text "Letter from Birmingham City Jail," says that he walks past the white churches and sees their steeples spiraling toward heaven and he wonders who is their God.

Un-reading the text creates a counter-text to the dominant text. And the sermon must be a manifestation and action against the dominant text, whether that is "experience" remembered and practiced or whether that dominant text is amnesia, as Walter Brueggemann describes it.[8] The election of Donald Trump by the evangelicals in America, if it does nothing else, should enable Black folk to remember their mistreatment, to remember injustice, and yes to remember the chains and shackles of four hundred years of slavery. It should remind Black folk of the struggles of Sojourner Truth, Harriet Tubman, Jarena Lee, and Fannie Lou Hamer—freedom fighters who died at the hands of those who daily invoked the name of the Lord. This remembrance must be accompanied by a hope and action that mitigate against depression and defeat of the human spirit. As long as we have an openness to both memory and hope, we can preach with greater clarity and conviction. We can preach more dangerously to the self and to the powers that be—whether in the church, the schools, the community, the family, or in the wider public square.[9]

Reading and Un-reading the Text

While Roland Barthes says that the true place of writing is reading,[10] I say, for the poor and oppressed, that the true place of writing is not reading but un-reading. The author writes only when he or she finishes reading and begins to un-read. Un-reading is an act of freedom and liberation for the oppressed and is the third part of the preaching process: reading, re-reading, un-reading, writing, and re-writing. Indeed, one's writing at this stage is the manifestation of one's ability to un-read.

---

8. See Walter Brueggemann, *The Word that Redescribes the World* (Minneapolis: Fortress, 2006), 3–19.

9. See Frank Thomas, *How to Preach A Dangerous Sermon* (Nashville: Abingdon Press, 2018).

10. See Barthes, *Image-Music-Text*, 140.

Writing follows un-reading. Un-reading is an act of rebellion, suspicion, and an act of freedom. Like love, un-reading is a revolution.[11] It is a critical interpretation and exegetical exercise in evaluating the hegemonic halo that has been placed over the text by centuries of scholars and interpreters who seek to construct a god whose image is a reflection of the self—the predominantly Eurocentric self—and then to instantiate this understanding in scripture and the biblical canon.

To couple reading with un-reading is a way of facing head-on the inherent assumptions of power and sovereignty that reside in the culture and in an array of biblical texts. Michael J. Gorman, in discussing biblical exegesis, makes an important statement that begs to be developed and expanded. He says that "the text is read and then 'unread' as a means of naming and being freed from oppression."[12] There you have it. To un-read the text is to recognize the hegemonic influences embedded in the scripture text. These influences of empire and colonialist ideology need to be called out, challenged, and confronted, and this can only be achieved through reading and re-reading critically, and then questioning or challenging the text through the clear lens of suspicion, mistrust, and critical analysis. This results in the un-reading of the text, which is a type of compassionate interrogation of the text that the poor and oppressed must do if they ever intend to be free. It is to confront and change the prescribed language of the text. It is to recognize the intertextuality of the text.

Every text is encumbered by something other than itself. Something other than what you see and read. African-American preachers cannot depend on the written text, nor any of its *glossia*, to free them willfully without struggle and challenge. This struggle to be free is a part of the social and cultural exegesis and interpretation process, which includes un-reading. Some stalwarts of the status quo may prefer to call this *eisegesis*, intending to suggest that exegesis is a type of pure, presupposition-less endeavor, which is a far cry from truth and honesty. In fact, there could be nothing further from the truth. Nothing in the Bible or theology is so pure

---

11. See Søren Kierkegaard, *Fear and Trembling, and the Sickness Unto Death* (Garden City, NY: Doubleday, 1954).

12. Michael J. Gorman, *Elements of Biblical Exegesis: A Basic Guide for Students and Ministers* (Grand Rapids, MI: Baker Academic, 2009), 22.

that it is without presuppositions. I contend that exegesis itself is a type of structured eisegesis inasmuch as it makes an axis through the experience of the exegete and a whole host of interpreters before him or her. And the way exegesis is done by biblical scholars, both Black and white, tends to perpetuate the status quo and privilege the past rather than advance a new world.

Yes, reading and re-reading are necessary prerequisites to un-reading, and this means that one has to read the text so well that un-reading is both creative and liberating, and that is made possible by what I call the *first reading* and the *first writing*. In other words, the preacher can only un-read the already-read just like he or she can only say more clearly the already-said. This is critical because there is so much in a text of which the reader should be suspicious and the scripture text is no exception. By suspicion, I mean skeptical and unwilling to accept something—anything—without question. Un-reading becomes an exegetical, homiletical, and theological interpretation tool for understanding a text more fully and creatively, culturally and contextually. To un-read is to understand the text in a language (semantics) or terministic screen other than the "tissue-thin" words of the writer, that is, to understand in your own written and spoken way of expressing meaning and understanding.

Un-reading is a higher, more creative form of reading that has made an axis through reading over and over again to the point of skepticism, suspicion, and doubt. These are necessary prerequisites to understanding and determining the meaning of the text. In fact, this helps the preacher to get in front of the text in a way that some Black preachers have done so masterfully. Ordinary traditional exegesis is designed primarily to get behind the text and not in front of it, as I have maintained. This means that it becomes virtually impossible to advocate and implement transformation from the vantage point of the past or from behind. Un-reading the text frees the text from its past transgressions or recognizes and confronts these transgressions and allows the preacher to pursue a proleptic vision of the text as an instrument of transformation and freedom. This keeps the text fresh and formative—almost approaching it as a type of text that is always in the process of becoming, creating, and recreating itself for every new context and new generations of preachers and interpreters of the word.

Un-reading is to resist the oppressive language of the text through any means necessary in the spirit of Malcolm X—deconstructing, re-contextualizing, reconstructing, refiguring, and re-describing the text with an eye toward freedom and love of the word. So, as a practice, one of the most unrestrictive and pragmatic ways for the preacher to get in front of the text is to un-read the text as a way of allowing the text to shed itself of the hegemonic elements that shaped its synchronic structure from the beginning.

How to Un-read the Scripture Text

Un-reading the text is not the antithesis of reading; rather it is the "be-yondness" of reading after re-reading *ad infinitum*. In going beyond the initial reading and re-reading of the text, un-reading becomes the ultimate form of reading that any reader can do in particularizing the chosen text. This is not about generalizing, but rather about making the text help to interpret itself, probably to the chagrin of its classical interpreters, especially the Hebrews and the Greeks. The deeper meaning of the text is achieved when the text is allowed to reveal itself in the un-reading manifested in the rewording or re-languaging of the text by the oppressed. The Black preacher and the Black Church continue to maintain a commitment to the text, but not in its existing canonical or hegemonic form, neither etymologically, semantically, or theologically.

Key words in the text lead to key concepts, which means that the preacher needs to identify all of the key words in the chosen text. These key words can be large or small, and the "sense" of each of them has to be identified to determine if they constitute the language of hegemony, colonization, oppression, injustice, or racism. We can surmise that there will be elements of some semblance of negativity embedded in these texts.

I am using the language of a homiletician and a linguistic philosopher, being fully aware that biblical scholars like Boykin Sanders, Robert Wafawanaka, and Yung Suk Kim, all part of the faculty at Virginia Union University, may argue that the language and logic of Jesus is a continuation of Torah, especially in the Gospel of Matthew when he says, "You have heard it said of old, but I say to you. You have heard it said that you should love your neighbor, and hate your enemy but I say unto you 'Love your enemies'" (Matt 5:43-44). Sanders wants to say that this language of Jesus intensifies Torah and catapults it to its logical and responsible conclusion. However, I am saying that there are other possibilities and other expectations. And the preacher has the freedom and the imagination—even the obligation—to be unbound by traditional and accepted interpretation or commentary.

Jesus provides the model for the un-reading of the text that I am talking about, which is seen throughout the Gospel of Matthew and also in the Gospels of Luke and John. Jesus's own teaching and preaching is often an un-reading, a re-reading, and re-writing of Torah. We see throughout the Gospel of Matthew Jesus quoting what the people had heard or read, but he refigures and re-describes their hearing and un-reads what they had heard. For example, Matthew 5 says,

> You have heard that it was said, "An eye for an eye and a tooth for a tooth."
> But I say to you, "Do not resist an evildoer...." You have heard that it was
> said, "You shall love your neighbor and hate your enemy." But I say to you,
> "Love your enemies and pray for those who persecute you, so that you may
> be children of your Father in heaven; for he makes his sun rise on the evil
> and on the good, and sends rain on the righteous and on the unrighteous."
> (v. 38-39, 43-45 NRSV)

Likewise, Jesus in Luke 6:35 encourages us to love our enemies:

> "...love your enemies, do good and lend, expecting nothing in return. Your
> reward will be great, and you will be children of the Most High..." (NRSV).

Tina Turner, with her mega triple-platinum number-one hit song "What's Love Got to Do with It," was being sarcastic. Yes, *love* has everything to do with it, according to the scripture. Jesus' words "love your enemies" seems like an oxymoron, a *non sequitur*, an illogical statement. Love your enemies—because we are so familiar with the love commandment "Love your neighbor as yourself" and even that seems virtually impossible, does it not? Love your neighbor is often thought to be connected to spatial proximity: the person across the street, the person next door, the person two or three doors down or on the next street over. These are all our neighbors. But can we love them in the same way that we love ourselves?

"Love your neighbor as yourself" seems to be an impossible task. Does that mean that you forgive your neighbor in the way that you forgive yourself? Are we ever as understanding and helpful to others as we are to the self, or is our neighbor always cut short because we do not see the self as Other? We see the self as self, as sacred and the other as Other—not as valuable, not as sacred, not as adept as the self. Is it not contrary to the way we think, the way we are taught, and the way we are socialized to love our neighbor as ourselves? The self is so centered in itself that the Other, the neighbor, is virtually excluded. Let us know from the start that the neighbor is everybody except the self—we are all neighbors because we are all Others—apart from the self, the ego, the me, my, mine, the *ich*.

A friend of mine called me to ask me what he should do because their neighbor, one who lives on the same street, had called her husband's job to report that the city vehicle he drove as a part of his job was taking up too much space on the street in front of his house. So he, the neighbor, called the man's job to drag his supervisor into the issue—an issue grounded in his egotism, excluding him from his neighbor. And a few days later, the neighbor placed a note on their car, saying they were parked too close to his driveway, and they should move their car. They called me because they felt harassed by their neighbor. I told them to go and talk to him about it for the umpteenth time and to let him know that the street is public property that belongs to all citizens equally. And neighbors have to learn to tolerate and respect each other.

Notice I did not say that they had to love one another like the Golden Rule, the ethics of responsibility teaches us. "Love your neighbor as yourself." But wait. That is hard. That is very difficult. That is a real challenge. We have trouble loving our neighbor. We cannot even decide who our neighbor really is—much less love them. But if you think loving the neighbor is hard, consider the text that says, "Love your enemies, do good and lend expecting nothing in return. Your reward will be great, and you will be children of the Most High; for he is kind to the ungrateful and the wicked. Be merciful just as your Father is merciful" (Luke 6:35-36 NRSV).

The Golden Rule is not enough because Jesus provides a new ethical and social standard, which is an un-reading of Torah. Loving your neighbor as yourself is not even enough, as hard as it may be. Jesus sets a new interpretation: *Love your enemies.* That is the meaning of *love*, if Kierkegaard is right saying that "love is a revolution." Jesus provides a new reading, a re-reading, and an *un-reading* of Torah.

Actions speak louder than words. Do good to those who hate you. Show the haters some love. Do not let "hateration" hinder you from doing good. *Hate* is a strong word, but when folk hate you, when the only thing they can say about you is negative, do good to them. When they get sick, visit them. When they need a reference letter, write something nice. When they stab you in the back, take the dagger out, sew up the wound, and keep on doing good.

Bless those who curse you, and pray for those who scorn you. This is what Jesus requires. If you are hated by folk in the church, in the street, in the university, in the community—love them! If you are scorned, talked bad about, called names, reviled, and cursed—if you are, in fact, hated—then love, love, love. In Martina McBride's popular song "Anyway," she sings, "You can love someone with all your heart for all the right reasons. They may choose to walk away. Love 'em anyway." We must love anyway.

It is not good enough to love those who love you. It is not good enough to scratch somebody's back because they scratch yours. It is not good enough to offer a *quid pro quo*, a tit for tat, a blessing for a blessing. No! What sort of credit is that to you? Even sinners can do that. Beloved, your standard is not the Golden Rule. Your standard is not yourself, and your standard is not a *minimalist* ethic. Your standard is to do as God would do.

JESUS: Writing on the Ground and the Act of Un-reading

The scribes and the Pharisees brought a woman who had been caught in adultery and making her stand before all of them, they said to him, "Teacher, this woman was caught in the very act of committing adultery. Now what do

*you say?" They said this to test him, so that they might have some charge to
bring against him. Jesus bent down and wrote with his finger on the ground.
When they kept on questioning him, he straightened up and said to them, "Let
anyone among you who is without sin be the first to throw a stone at her."
And once again he bent down and wrote on the ground.*

—John 8:1-11

We all understand what it means to be accused by those who are no
less guilty, and by implication, no more righteous than we are. Indeed, it is
the nature of the human being to be flawed to the point of failure, flawed
by fault—by the chasm that separates us from God, though we are made
in God's image. We know and subscribe to an ethic that says that adultery
is one of the high crimes and misdemeanors both in scripture and in society. People treat it as one of the unforgivables, the non-negotiables, the
last straw among married couples, and yet in this text, adultery is trumped
by grace, mercy, and love as a result of Jesus's *un-reading* of the Torah text
and his writing on the ground.

We are seemingly so self-righteous, so full of it, that we become an
intolerable law unto ourselves. In a sense, we are all liars and cheats; we are
potentially as crooked and conniving as the next person. Sin is not something that we can escape, except through death. But, for that matter, neither can we escape grace. Indeed, "where sin increased, grace multiplied
even more" (Rom 5:20). I am a witness and I am a living exhibition of
this dialectic of sin and grace. We all are! I believe that Jesus is the embodiment and the fulfillment of both law and grace. Herein lies our hope and
our second chances. And this text provides the example for our reading,
re-reading, un-reading, writing, and re-writing.

I am more than troubled and disturbed by the fact that in the church,
in the family, and in the culture, we have become so self-righteous, so
much the sovereign self, that this false "holier than thou" sacral person has
brought an end to relationships and marriages with children. "He cheated
on me." "She cheated on me." "He violated our sacred vows, our bond."
"She stepped out on me."

Euripides, a Greek playwright and peer of Sophocles, dramatized a
tragedy of a woman who gets away with murder all because her husband

violated the contract of marriage. *Medea* is the story of a woman scorned who rewarded her husband's infidelity with the death of his soon-to-be bride, his soon-to-be father-in-law, and even the death of their own children, conceived during happier times. Well, read the Bible sometimes. Study the word. Listen to the preacher, hear the sermon, and try to get past your own Greek, Victorian, and Romanticist ideology.

In this Johannine text, the teachers of the law and the Pharisees—the preachers, the deacons, and the trustees, the elders of the church—bring to Jesus a woman who was "caught in the act of adultery"—naked, dress over her head, caught in the act. Wow! The text does not say anything about her male lover. We can infer that patriarchy prevails, and he got up, walked away, and was never accused. But this nameless woman here in the text is brought to Jesus so that he could pronounce judgment on her—life or death, according to the law of Moses. "Teacher, this woman was caught in the act of adultery. In the law, Moses commanded us to stone such women. Now what do you say?"

Jesus says nothing at all. And yet, in his deafening silence, he says it all. He does not say a mumbling word. No yapping. No ethical treatise. No recapitulating of the law, list of violations and codes, lecture on fidelity and faith, on faults and failures. No speeches. No sermons. No chastising. No cussing and fussing. No banishing the woman to the downstairs "couch," to the courts, to the marriage and family therapists, to the addiction counselors!

Jesus gave no divorce decree, no separation papers, no reiteration of the law, no moralizing, and no display of stress and strain. Jesus did not say a word—not a thing. Instead of speaking, "he bent down and wrote on the ground with his finger." His writing on the ground is an act of sovereign silence, which itself is an un-reading of the text. The symbolism is great here. Bending down and writing on the ground is an act of un-reading the law—a law that he knew so well. When he wrote on the ground, he could have written "Where is the man?" or he could have written "Where is justice?" or "Where is fairness?" So much for Leviticus 20:10 and Deuteronomy 22:23-24.

133

I know that various New Testament texts have Jesus saying that he has not come to abolish the law, but to fulfill it (cf. Matt 5:17-20). And yet I say with some degree of skepticism and assurance (and a heap of respect for the learned biblical scholars), that Jesus's words as he bent over and wrote on the ground is an abolishing of the law in a sense. A type of *refiguring* of the law. A reconstruction of the law. This is a re-reading of the Torah and an un-reading of the law and an un-reading of Leviticus 20:10. This is a re-writing of the law precisely because he (Jesus) embodies the law, and the fact that he personifies the dialectic of law and grace enables him to un-read the law (in this case, the Leviticus text) and re-write the law right there on the spot, on the ground of the temple in the presence of the purveyors of the sacrality of the law.

This is awesome. This is radical. This is transformative. This is cataclysmic. This is revolutionary. This is the meaning of interpretation and preaching the gospel. This is philosophical and theological hermeneutics in action. It is the taking of the Torah texts and un-reading them and then embodying this reconstruction, this postmodern deconstruction into a second reading—re-reading, a new reading, a new interpretation that is now, for all practical purposes, an *un-reading* of the Torah text. And Jesus's bending down is a physical action laden with semiotics and symbolism that itself points to something meaningful and dramatic that is either profound and perfunctory or both. Either way, his action is laden with meaning and the power of writing on the ground is an act of un-reading and re-writing texts.

> "Teacher, this woman was caught in the very act of committing adultery. Now in the law Moses commanded us to stone such a woman. Now what do you say?" [. . .] Jesus bent down and wrote on the ground with his finger. When they kept on questioning him, he straightened up and said to them, "Let anyone among you who is without sin be the first to throw a stone at her." And once again he bent down and wrote on the ground. (John 8:4-8 NRSV)

Jesus writes on the ground a second time following his challenge to the scribes and Pharisees, the teachers of the law. Anyone of you can be first to participate in this woman's death by stoning. Remember now that they made her stand before the group as they accused her, but Jesus's directive was like polling the jury where one has to step up and own his own verdict and actions. No more hiding behind the group. Group psychology is a monster, an obviation of identity and an obfuscation of responsibility. Jesus's statement mitigated against any of the teachers of the law and Pharisees shielding themselves behind one another. Each person had to search his own heart and soul, because Jesus, after bending down and writing on the ground the first time, after being taunted and interrogated, decided to read and *un-read* what he had written, to interpret his own writing.

Jesus offers a conditional if-then statement, a logical syllogism. If A, then B. If not A, then not B. The statement demanded a searching of the self, a coming to grips with the unrighteous and unholy self, the self subjected to the same scrutiny under which they had placed the woman. The statement is piercing and palpable. It is pointed. It stops you in your tracks; it jolts you to a new level of consciousness; it smacks you upside the head like a left hook from Muhammad Ali.

Jesus's writing on the ground is a gesture of disinterest toward the scribes and teachers of the law's self-importance and judgmental character. They too are from the dirt, the dust of the earth. It is in a sense a fundamental act of defiance regarding their interpretation of law and their hermeneutic arrogance—an arrogance that still hovers over the heads of some modern-day teachers of the law, biblical scholars whose theories of explanation are quite confounding to me. To wit, there is very little in the literature to help me with my interpretation of John 8:1-11. As a matter of fact, biblical scholars and commentators simply omit it from their explication with the blatant assertion that it does not even belong in John's Gospel, so it should be shunned as if it does not exist. Stanley B. Marrow asserts, "As a matter of fact it fits more neatly after, e.g., Luke 21:38 than it does between John 7:52 and 8:12, where it merely interrupts Jesus' discourse at the feast of Tabernacles."[13] But they can say what they will. As I have stated before, we need to be suspicious of commentary. You will never think for yourself as long as you are a slave to Matthew Henry's *Bible Commentary*, the *Interpreter's Bible Commentary*, and so forth.

---

13. See Stanley B. Marrow, *The Gospel of John: A Reading* (New York: Paulist, 1995), 124.

"Let anyone among you who is without sin be the first to throw a stone at her" (v. 7 NRSV). This statement by Jesus hurts the ego with its inordinate and unsurpassed bold confrontation of the judgmental self—a self-unknown until it is pierced by the statement Jesus posed. This statement makes Jesus both prosecutor and defense attorney. Could that be what he wrote on the ground with his finger? Could this be the embodiment of the reading, re-reading, un-reading, writing, and re-writing of the law and the un-reading of the Leviticus and Deuteronomy texts? And after Jesus said this, the scripture text says that "And once again he bent down and wrote on the ground" (v. 8 NRSV). It is like he tuned all of them out. The noise of their accusations, mumblings, and murmurings was reduced to nothing. To silence. Jesus finessed them into silence, the result of a new conviction. A new ethic. A new theology and the creation of a new world.

This second writing could have been an editing of what he wrote the first time. It could have been an erasure of the first writing. He could have drawn a line through it. He could have bluffed them, or he could have written their names one by one and beside each name, he could have written stuff that they thought was hidden and unknown. Whatever he wrote on the ground, it was apparently very powerful, pointed, and painfully piercing as "when they heard it, they went away one by one, beginning with the elders" (v. 9 NRSV). I think the key here is the writing on the ground the second time: "*And once again* he bent down and wrote on the ground" and "When they heard it, they went away..." In other words, it is this un-reading, this re-writing, that causes them to disperse. Yes, they heard what Jesus said, but they did not move. It was after he bent down and wrote on the ground the second time that they began to go away. At this. At this second *writing*. At this particular *writing*, those who heard began to go away. This is amazing. This is almost unreal. This is mind-boggling.

Those committed to the law, that is, those devoted to Torah, the scribes and Pharisees, were masters of teaching, interpreting, and enforcing the law—a law that clearly stated "you shall bring both of them to the gate of that town and stone them to death" (Deut 22:24 NRSV) and "if a man commits adultery with a married woman...both the adulterer and the adulteress must be executed" (Lev 20:10). And yet, in the face of Jesus, nobody could throw a stone at her. These architects and practitioners of the law were eyewitnesses to the violation of their own law. Remember that John 8:1-6 says that they caught her in the very act of adultery, so that truth was apparently stipulated and uncontested by everybody—the woman, the teachers of the law, the Pharisees, the scribes, and Jesus. It was so. Incontrovertible. Let it be. Let it be understood as truth. It is the truth according to the law, and yet they could not carry out the indictment of the very law that they cherished and practiced.

The text says that they walked away. Every one of them. Jetted. Bolted. Disappeared. Silenced. Muted. Messed up by the writing on the ground. It was the writing on the ground, written by the finger of love and forgiveness. The writing on the ground, written by the finger of Jesus—a finger of peace and understanding. It was the writing on the ground, written by the finger of Jesus—a finger of transparency and tranquility. The writing on the ground edited by the master editor who edited out words like *guilt* and *shame* from my life and your life. Yes, in writing on the ground, Jesus edited out our sins, wrote a line through them, and where there was a guilty verdict, Jesus wrote "not guilty." Where there was hate, he wrote "love." Where there was weakness, he wrote "strength." Where there was sickness, he wrote "healed."

Let us walk away from judging folk because of their faults and failures. Let us walk away from those who are in the crowd ready to condemn and convict somebody for what they have done wrong. The writing is not on the wall. This time the writing is on the ground.

"Go," Jesus said to the woman, "and do not sin again." Go from this day forward and do something with your life. Go, and be faithful. Go, and show mercy to somebody else. Go *and...* Do not just go like nothing happened. No, Go *and.* You do not just go away from here like you have never been here at this place. No, go and fix yourself up. Go, and be a witness to the love, mercy, and grace of God.

SOME SUGGESTED OLD TESTAMENT TEXTS FOR "UN-READING"

Genesis

1:26-28—Creation of male and female as equals

2:18-25—Creation of man and woman as partners

16:1-16—Hagar, Sarah, and Abraham. Who wields the power?

19—Lot's daughters. Who is in control?

20:1-18—Abraham and Abimelech. When is lying sanctioned?

22:1-24—The binding of Isaac (the Akedah). Would you do it?

30:24-23—Jacob cheats Laban

38—Judah and Tamar. The revenge of the impugned woman!

39:1-23—Joseph and Potiphar's wife. The good boy and bad mistress?

Exodus

1–2—State-sanctioned murder and the birth of Moses

32:1-29—The Golden Calf. Who is to blame, and why?

Leviticus

18–19—What is truly abominable? Can we afford to cherry-pick?

Numbers

22–24—Balaam narrative. Who is in control?

Deuteronomy

7:1-16—The law of the *herem*. Who should be destroyed? The problem of holy warfare.

22–23—On more legal injunctions

Joshua

2:1-7—Rahab. Whose side is she on? Heroine or sellout?

2:1–11:23—How do we read the narratives of Joshua?

Judges

4–5—Is murder through deceit justified? Is violence to be celebrated and called "blessed"?

11:1-40—The daughter of Jephthah and rash vows. Do we make some?

13:1–16:31—Samson and his appetites. How do we read him?

19:1-30—The Levite's unnamed concubine and the violence done to her. What is the moral?

Ruth

3:1-18—Naomi, Ruth, and Boaz. How do we read them? What really happened?

1 Samuel

13:1-23—Rejection of Saul. Did he really deserve it? What about David (2 Sam 11–12)?

15:1-35—Saul, the Amalekites, and holy war ideology. Is this a moral guide for us?

2 Samuel

1:17-27—David's eulogy of Saul and Jonathan. Why should he have cared?

11:1–12:30—Covetousness, adultery, deceit, murder...why is David still king?

1 Kings

11:1-41—The sins of Solomon and division of the kingdom. Was Solomon that legendary?

21:1-29—Jezebel's murder of Naboth. Where was the king?

2 Kings

11:1-20—A queen in Israel? How is she viewed? Where are the other queens?

21:1-26—Why do really bad kings like Manasseh rule for so long?

22–23—Why do really good kings like Josiah die so young?

1 Chronicles

10:1-14—The evaluation of Saul's kingship. Was he that bad?

2 Chronicles

5:11–7:7—Temple dedication ceremony. What a ceremony! Why?

33:1-15—Was Manasseh not so bad after all?

Ezra

1:1–6:22—Return from exile. Who funds you, and who controls you?

Nehemiah

10–13—Nehemiah's law and assimilation issues. What are we to do?

13:1-31—Nehemiah: separatist or reformer? A moral guide for us?

Esther

1:1-21—On Persian banquets. What do we learn? Who eats and who doesn't?

1:1–2:23—Vashti and Esther. How do we read them?

Tobit

How do we show hospitality and acts of kindness?

Judith

12–15—Murder of Holofernes. Are deceit and murder ever justifiable?

16:1-25—Are violent acts to be celebrated? Is Judith a heroine or a murderer?

Job

1:1–2:13—When bad things happen to good people. What about Job's wife?

42:1-17—What is the moral of the story?

Psalms

51–71—What are we to do with lament psalms? What do we learn?

137—What are we to do with imprecatory psalms? Religiously sanctioned violence?

Proverbs

4:1-27—The two ways. How do we choose in a seductive culture?

31:10-31—The ideal wife. Whose ideal? Whose wife? What does she say?

Ecclesiastes

1:1–2:26—Is everything we are doing really vanity and worthless?

11:7–12:1-8—What do we learn about youth and old age? Is this wisdom?

Song of Solomon

1:5-6—What color was Solomon's bride? What do translations say? Why?

1–8—How do we preach from a love-filled text? Why was this book canonized?

Wisdom of Solomon
What are the influences of Stoic and Platonic philosophical principles in this book?

Wisdom of Ben Sirach (Ecclesiasticus)
22:1-27—Are Sirach's views on women redeemable today? Was he a misogynist?

25:10-26—More of Sirach on women. Really?

42:1-25—More of Sirach on women. Wow!

Isaiah
7–8—The meaning of the Immanuel sign. What did it mean? What does it mean?

Jeremiah
7:1-15—Temple sermon. What do we learn about proper worship? Is being religious enough?

26:1-6—Temple sermon. What else do we learn about worship and social responsibility?

Lamentations
1–5—What do we learn about lamenting? How do we deal with a violent and enemy-like God?

Ezekiel
14:12-20—On individual responsibility. What else does the Bible say?

37:1-14—The valley of dry bones. What hope do we have?

Baruch
1:1-22—Do we still confess our sins? Is punishment always due to sin?

Hosea
1–3—What kind of God sanctions this behavior and these names?

Joel

2:28-29—Who should prophesy or preach? Why do some chuches not ordain women?

Amos

5:18-24—What is proper worship? How do we worship? What is justice and righteousness?

Obadiah

Should we celebrate the fall of our enemies? Are enemies universal?

Jonah

1:2–2:11—Do we have a choice of whom we preach to? Are we xenophobic?

Micah

6:6-8—What really does the Lord require?

Nahamiah

1:1-8—How do we handle the wrath of the Lord? Is violence justifiable?

Habidiah

2:2-3—What is the vision to write down and make plain?

Zephaniah

1:1–2:3—What did the Day of the Lord mean for Judah? For us?

Haggai

1:1-11—Why was temple building delayed? What are our priorities?

Zechariah

8:1-8—Vision of a restored city and people. Is it realistic?

Malachia

3:8-10—How are we robbing God today?

Daniel

1:1-21—Should we bow down to empire?

1–6—Can God still deliver us from oppression?

7–12—What hope is there for oppressed people in Daniel's apocalyptic visions?

1 Maccabees

2:1-70—Should Christians resist empire as the Maccabees and Masada Jews did?

2 Maccabees

6:18–7:42—Is *martyrdom* a viable option? What does that mean today? What is the nexus of religion and politics in the Bible and in our world? Do the two meet? How should we read ancient religious texts and concepts in a modern context? Are they sufficient moral guidelines for us? How should we read them? How authoritative are these texts today?

A p p e n d i x   B

SOME SUGGESTED NEW TESTAMENT TEXTS FOR "UN-READING"

METHOD: Read, RE-Read, UN-Read these scriptures from the NRSV translation. Successful re-reading of the text allows us to *unread*; this creates fulcrum to unleash imagination, vision, and radicalism from the text. *Un-reading* allows us to achieve freedom from the intention of the text/scripture.

Matthew

10:19—Was this activist preparation/training like the sit-ins, or divination of Christ's responses to his persecutors prior to crucifixion?

18:20—Christ as the "word/name" makes one—and one individual make two, therefore —we are never alone; Or triune—Father/Son/ Holy Spirit make three, therefore (I am) Christ is ever-present.

Mark

5:21-34—Who is the Christ figure in the text? How can this text be related to gender equality?

Mark 14:7—This text, on the face of it, is the paradigm of absurdity, assigning an eternal status to poor people.

Luke

10:25-37—Was this an illustration which emphasizes the "goodness" of the Samaritan—or the "wickedness" of the others? Considering the contextual relationship of the Samaritan community—even

147

the Samaritan was a "Good Enemy." Expound of the transient nature of "goodness" and "wickedness" embedded in this text.

Were the Priest/Levite simply unable to help due to lack of resources/strength? There is an intrinsic enablement through the employment of resources [i.e. *denarii*, bandages, oil/wine, animal/transportation, confidence in community influence via innkeeper]?

John

10:16—How are Christians to relate to other faith traditions? How might decentering Christianity create a more inclusive environment?

14:13-14—*Anything* is not everything. Expound on differences here. There are parameters that remain inherent to "anything" here.

20:29—Explore *faith* versus *evidence*; Is this text suggesting blind or haphazard discipleship with Christ? Is this setting up a hierarchy within beliefs?

Acts

5:1-11—Unread this story of Ananias and his wife. Integrity and honesty are valued above human-life. Is this text demonstrative of grace, mercy, and/or forgiveness? Where is grace in the text? Why did Peter not forewarn her? Where was her "church community" to help her (the wife)? With 4:36-37 included, this narrative positions the "covet" of Barnabas's esteem with the Apostle.

Romans

9:16—Is salvation universal?

1 Corinthians

1:13-15, 10:23, 14:22—Are we to understand that Crispus/Gaius *can* respond differently—because they were baptized by Paul?

14:33b-36—The subjugation of women.

Galatians

5:1-15—What is the nature of Christian freedom? In a white, racist society, what is freedom for Black people?

Ephesians

6:5, 9—Is slavery compatible with the gospel of Jesus Christ?

Philippians

4:8, 4:13—What good things ought to be the center of our thoughts?

1 Timothy

6:1—The issue of slavery.

Philemon

1:10—Paul's plea to free Onesimus from prison.

Hebrews

13:5—A response to a materialistic culture.

James

5:12—How can a person be free if they cannot say "yes" or "no"?

1 Peter

2:13—The authority of human governments.

1 John

2:7-8—A commandment to love.

Revelation

21:1-8—A vision of a new heaven and the new earth. How are we to envision Christian social transformation?

BIBLIOGRAPHY

Adler, Mortimer J. *How to Read a Book: The Classic Guide to Intelligent Reading*. New York: Touchstone, 1972.

Arendt, Hannah. *Eichmann in Jerusalem: A Report on the Banality of Evil*. New York: Penguin Books, 1963.

Austin, John L. *Philosophical Papers*. Oxford: Clarendon, 1961.

———. *Sense and Sensibilia*. London: Oxford University Press, 1962.

Baldwin, James. *Go Tell It on the Mountain*. New York: Vintage Books, 1952.

Barthes, Roland. *Image-Music-Text*. New York: Hill and Wang, 1977.

———. *The Pleasure of the Text*. New York: Hill and Wang, 1975.

———. *The Rustle of Language*. Berkeley: University of California Press, 1986.

Benjamin, Walter. *Illuminations: Essays and Reflections*. New York: Schocken Books, 1968.

Bonhoeffer, Dietrich. *The Cost of Discipleship*. New York: Macmilllian, 1959.

Booth, Stephen, ed. *Shakespeare's Sonnets*. New Haven, CT: Yale University Press, 2000.

Bouchard, Larry. (Professor, Religious Studies, University of Virginia), in discussion with the author, July 20, 2011.

Bruce, F. F. *Hard Sayings of Jesus*. Downers Grove, IL: InterVarsity, 1983.

Cone, James H. *The Cross and the Lynching Tree*. Maryknoll, NY: Orbis Books, 2011.

Cosgrove, Charles H., and W. Dow Edgerton. *In Other Words: Incarnational Translation for Preaching*. Grand Rapids, MI: Eerdmans, 2007.

Craddock, Fred B. *Preaching*. Nashville: Abingdon Press, 1985.

Derrida, Jacques, and T. Patrick Mensah, trans. *Monolingualism of the Other, or The Prosthesis of Origin*. Stanford: Stanford University Press, 1998.

———, and Anne Dufourmantelle, trans. *Of Hospitality*. Stanford: Stanford University Press, 2000.

Dickinson, Emily, and E. Martha Dickinson Bianchi. *The Complete Poems of Emily Dickinson*. Boston: Little, Brown and Company, 1924.

Didion, Joan. *Blue Nights*. New York: Vintage International, 2011.

Eliot, T. S. *Four Quartets*. New York: Harcourt, Brace and Company, 1943.

Fagles, Robert T., trans. *Homer: The Odyssey*. New York: Penguin, 2006.

Forster, E. M. *A Passage to India*. New York: Harcourt, Brace and Company, 1924.

Gorman, Michael J. *Elements of Biblical Exegesis*. Grand Rapids, MI: Baker Academic, 2009.

Gutiérrez, Gustavo. *A Theology of Liberation*. Maryknoll, NY: Orbis Books, 1973.

Hanh, Thich Nhat. *The Art of Communicating*. New York: Harper One, 2013.

Harris, James H. *No Longer Bound.* Eugene, OR: Cascade Books, 2013.

———. *Preaching Liberation.* Minneapolis: Fortress, 1996.

———. *The Word Made Plain.* Minneapolis: Fortress, 2006.

Hicks, H. Beecher. *Preaching Through a Storm.* Valley Forge, PA: Judson, 1976.

Hurston, Zora Neale. *Jonah's Gourd Vine.* New York: Harper Perennial, 1934.

Iser, Wolfgang. *The Act of Reading: A Theory of Aesthetic Response.* Baltimore: Johns Hopkins University Press, 1978.

———. *Prospecting: From Reader Response to Literary Anthropology.* Baltimore: Johns Hopkins University Press, 1989.

Jakobson, R. "Linguistics and Poetics." *Style in Language.* Ed. T. Sebeok. Cambridge: Massachusetts Institute of Technology Press, 1960, 350–377.

Jasper, J. R. *"De Sun Do Move." Reverend John Jasper.* Trans. John Bryan. Richmond: Charles Creek Pub., 2008.

Kafka, Franz. *The Metamorphosis and Other Stories.* New York: Dover, 1996.

Kaiser, Otto. *Isaiah 1–12.* The Old Testament Library. Philadelphia: Westminster, 1983.

Kierkegaard, Søren. *Fear and Trembling, and the Sickness Unto Death.* Garden City, NY: Doubleday, 1954.

LaRue, Cleophus. *The Heart of Black Preaching.* Louisville: Westminster John Knox, 2000.

Levine, Lawrence W. *Black Culture and Black Consciousness: Afro-American Folk Thought From Slavery to Freedom.* Oxford: Oxford University Press, 1977.

Limburg, James. *Hosea–Micah.* Interpretation: A Biblical Commentary for Teaching and Preaching. Louisville: Westminster John Knox, 1988.

Long, Thomas G. *Hebrews*. Interpretation: A Bible Commentary for Teaching and Preaching. Louisville: Westminster John Knox, 1997.

Melville, Herman. *Bartleby and Benito Cereno*. New York: Dover, 1990.

Mitchell, Henry H. *Black Preaching*. Nashville: Abingdon Press, 1990.

Muller-Volmer, Kurt. *The Hermeneutics Reader*. New York: Continuum, 2000.

The New Interpreter's Study Bible: New Revised Standard Version with the Apocrypha. Nashville: Abingdon Press, 2003.

Nussbaum, Martha. *Love's Knowledge: Essays on Philosophy and Literature*. New York: Oxford University Press, 1990.

Ochs, Peter. (Professor, Modern Judaic Studies, University of Virginia), in discussion with the author, October 13, 2016.

Parfit, Derek. *Reasons and Persons*. New York: Oxford University Press, 1984.

Peebles, James W., ed. *Winston's Original African Heritage Study Bible: Encyclopedia Concordance*. Nashville: James C. Winston, 1996.

Richards, I. A. *Beyond*. New York: Harcourt Brace Jovanovich, 1973.

———. *How to Read a Page: A Course in Efficient Reading with an Introduction to 100 Great Words*. Boston: Beacon, 1959.

Ricoeur, Paul. *From Text to Action: Essays in Hermeneutics, II*. Evanston: Northwestern University Press, 2017.

———. *Hermeneutics and Human Sciences*. Cambridge: Cambridge University Press, 1981.

———. *Intrepretation Theory: Discourse and the Surplus of Meaning*. Fort Worth: Texas Christian University Press, 1976.

————. "The Model of the Text: Meaningful Action Considered as a Text." *New Literary History* 5 (1973): 91–117.

————. *Time and Narrative, Vol. 1.* Chicago: University of Chicago Press, 1984.

Riddick, Dwight Shawrod II. *Dealing with Delay: Successful Living During Life's Layovers.* Suffolk: Final Step, 2016.

Robinson, Marilynne. *Gilead.* New York: Farrar, Straus and Giroux, 2004.

Segovia, Fernando F., and Mary Ann Tolbert, eds. *Reading from this Place, Vol. 1, Social Location and Biblical Interpretation in the United States.* Minneapolis: Fortress, 1995.

Shakespeare, William. *Hamlet.* Ed. Ann Thompson and Neil Taylor. New York: Bloomsbury, 2006.

Simmons, Martha J., and Frank A. Thomas, eds. *Preaching with Sacred Fire: An Anthology of African American Sermons, 1750 to the Present.* New York: Norton, 2010.

Smith, Patricia. *Incendiary Art: Poems.* Evanston: Northwestern University Press, 2017.

Stapleton, John Mason. *Preaching in Demonstration of the Spirit and Power.* Philadelphia: Fortress, 1988.

Thomas, Frank A. *How to Preach a Dangerous Sermon.* Nashville: Abingdon Press, 2018.

Thompson, Lisa L. *Ingenuity: Preaching as an Outsider.* Nashville: Abingdon Press, 2018.

Tillich, Paul. *The Eternal Now.* New York: Charles Scribner's Sons, 1963.

Valdes, Mario J., ed. *A Ricoeur Reader: Reflection and Imagination.* Toronto: University of Toronto Press, 1991.

Whitehead, Alfred North. *Process and Reality*. New York: Free Press, 1978.

Wilmore, Gayraud. *Black Religion and Black Radicalism: An Interpretation of the Religious History of African Americans*. Maryknoll, NY: Orbis Books, 1983.

Wilson, Walter E., ed. *The Selected Writings of W. E. B. Du Bois*. New York: New American Library, 1970.

Wright, Richard. *Black Boy*. New York: Harper Perennial, 1945.

Young, Robert. *Untying the Text*. New York: Routledge, 1990.

CPSIA information can be obtained
at www.ICGtesting.com
Printed in the USA
LVHW020622100919
630489LV00001B/1

9 781501 889066